Wanna Know a Truth?

Wanna Know a Truth?

— A SIMPLE MAN'S SEARCH FOR THE TRUTHS IN HIS LIFE —

Tony Garcia

Copyright © 2016 Tony Garcia
All rights reserved.

ISBN-13: 9781539896227
ISBN-10: 1539896226
Library of Congress Control Number: 2016918473
CreateSpace Independent Publishing Platform
North Charleston, South Carolina

Preface

I never fancied myself a writer. I merely began putting words to paper as a way to clear the thoughts in my head, for there were so many. As I shared these thoughts, others seemed to find a connection to my words as though the words were speaking directly to them, calling them out by name. I sense this comes from the common threads that all of humanity shares.

I never imagined myself as an author. I wanted only to share ideas that passed through me. As I wrote these ideas, others seemed awakened by the message as though the words nudged something into consciousness that had lain dormant. I sense this comes from our internal desire to feel completely alive.

I did not see brilliance or beauty in the words I wrote. I did not see them as poetry, although I admit a fondness for rhymes. I did not see depth or wisdom in the ideas once penned on the back of a napkin. I do not see these random musing as the possession of a gift.

The words are simple, reflecting the simple man behind them. The words are hopeful, reflecting the hope with which I walk. The words are gentle, reflecting a desire to bring peace to those reading my thoughts. The words are true, reflecting the story of a simple, hopeful, gentle man searching for his truth.

When I began writing, it seemed to be all about running. How the miles had gone, what was coming up in my schedule, goals I had set, races I had finished. The more I wrote and reflected, the more I realized I wasn't writing about running at all. It was simply about living and all that brings. I was merely using running as a metaphor, as a point of reference. So, as you read this book, you will find references to running or perhaps talk of miles. Yet this is not just for runners. I do not see it as a book about running.

So what follows in these pages? The day-to-day thoughts of one who views the world a little differently. The voice of one who speaks in hushed tones in hopes that others will quiet the noise to hear a story. The words of one who has been humbled by living. The story of one who believes in hope and faith, light and love, goodness and truth, peace and kindness, the dance and living life full force.

There have been tears shed along the way. It is possible that some words will bring tears. There have been so many, many smiles along the way. It is a hope that some words will bring smiles. There have been truths learned along the way. It is a hope that some words will resonate with your truth. And whether you read these words daily or pick this book up every now and again, I hope it will make a difference in that moment, whether it be inspiration, simple reflection, growth, or comfort.

Go get today. ~G

To Benjamin
For believing in my truths
For believing in me

January 1

We spend January 1st walking through our lives, room by room, drawing up a list of work to be done, cracks to be patched. Maybe this year, to balance the list, we ought to walk through the rooms of our lives...not looking for flaws, but for potential.
—Ellen Goodman*

It's not about January
Not another resolution
It's simply about me
Deciding to get it done

It's not about the calendar
Nor another new year
Do not need a reminder
To get myself in gear

It's not about the season
Nor a date soon to expire
Need not a single reason
To keep reaching higher

But if I must make a promise
A resolution for others to hear
Let it be as simple this:
Be good to myself this year

If that I can simply remember
Beyond the first of January
Then come next December
I will be where I want to be.

January 2

The best preparation for tomorrow is doing your best today.
—H. Jackson Brown Jr.

I called out unto Tomorrow with so many questions.

"Where will I be, Tomorrow?"

"Only as far as you are willing to travel today."

"Which direction shall the path lead, Tomorrow?"

"Only in the direction you turn today."

"What will I accomplish, Tomorrow?"

"Only that which you prepared for today."

"Who will I be, Tomorrow?"

"Only the person you forged today."

"How will I overcome the challenges, Tomorrow?"

"Only by getting stronger today."

"Tomorrow, why do you only speak of today?"

"Because the answers to all of your questions can be found today."

January 3

I am not me. I am not my body. I am my love, my kindness, and my service.
—Debasish Mridha

I am not a survivor. I am just a fighter.

I am not motivated. I am just disciplined.

I am not brave. I am just tired of being afraid.

I am not strong. I am just unwilling to choose weakness.

I am not flawless. I am just accepting of my imperfections.

I am not stubborn. I am just fiercely me.

I am not a superhero. I am just playing one in my own life.

I am not just anyone. I am completely me.

January 4

Blessed are the hearts that can bend; they shall never be broken.
—Albert Camus

In my weakest hour
Knowing I am beat
This now my only power
Simply rising to my feet

Heard fear's voice
As I was about to fall
This now my only choice
Choosing to stand tall

At the very edge of defeat
Life had gotten the best of me
Did not surrender or retreat
But raised my arms in victory

This now my defining moment
Truer words never spoken
Times I may have bent
But I shall not be broken.

January 5

When something comes easy, you usually let it go the same way.
—Nora Roberts

Easy taught me to swim downstream.

It never showed me how to rage against the current.

Easy had me turned toward the sunshine.

It never prepared me to face the looming storm.

Easy accepted all my excuses.

It never expected enough of me.

Easy said the status quo is good enough.

It never spoke a truth I needed to hear.

I did not come here for easy.

January 6

Feel yourself climbing the mountain.
—A. D. Posey

Stood before my mountain, cold and dark. Fearful of the climb, for it seemed so steep. Fearful of the climb, for there was no path. Yet climb I must, for what I knew waited on the other side.

Gathered my courage, summoned my strength, called upon my faith, and began to climb. Progress was slow, the struggle great, times I wanted to turn back around. Yet onward I climbed, for what I knew waited on the other side.

The climb took a toll. There were tears and scars and pain from the stumbles, missteps, and falls. I grew weary of the battle it seemed I could not win. Yet I continued to climb, for what I knew waited on the other side.

Finally neared the top of my mountain. Breathless, exhausted, broken. Found the will to scramble to the summit, exalted in victory, arms raised in triumph. For now I would gaze upon what I knew waited on the other side.

And as I stood atop my mountain, in the distance, all I could see were more mountains awaiting me. And as I made my way back down, gone was the fear.

For I finally learned the mountains ahead of me have already been conquered. I simply need to climb them.

January 7

I am not a superhero. I am just playing one in my own life.
—Tony Garcia

It is not arrogance.

It is an unwavering belief.

This is to truly trust yourself.

It is not the voice of another.

It is an inner whisper.

This is to truly know yourself.

It is not a reflection in the mirror.

It is an image carried within.

This is to truly see yourself.

It is not a false sense of pride.

It is an honest rejoicing.

This is to truly celebrate yourself.

It is not a gift granted a few.

It is the birthright of all.

This is to truly love yourself.

January 8

There is only one corner of the universe you can be certain of improving,
and that's your own self.
—Aldous Huxley

Ten Ways to Improve Your Own Self

1. Stop comparing yourself to others: Their story is not yours. Quit reading their autobiographies. Write your own.

2. Get outside yourself: Do something positive for someone else. It will change your perspective and get you out of your "woe is me" pattern of thinking.

3. Choose discipline over motivation or punishment: Discipline sets the alarm clock. Discipline gets you on the road. Discipline makes the right decisions. Motivation wanes. Motivation is a momentary fix. Motivation depends on external rewards. Punishment simply does not alter behavior long term.

4. Let go: The past. Your fears. The notion that you are not worthy. Your chains. The belief that failing is a given. Your excuses. All the stuff you hold on to that no longer serves your good.

5. Try something new: See #4. What if you actually let go? What if you said, "Why not me? Why not now?" I get it. Old habits die hard. Yeah, and there is a reason. You refuse to bury them. Do new.

6. Be your own superhero: OK, so I may not be able to save the world. OK, so I may not be Superman. I don't have to be. I simply have to understand that I am equipped with enough power to save myself.

7. Forgive yourself: See #3. Punishing yourself over could haves, should haves, would haves will change absolutely nothing—ever! Let yourself up.

8. Find peace where you stand: You are here—for whatever reason. Breathe. Relax. It does not have to be where you remain. But for now, it is a place from which to take stock. What needs to change? Where am I going? How do I get there? In those answers, find peace. And soon where you now stand shall be a place from which to launch yourself.

9. Know what you want: Quit waffling. Decide what is important to you. Be clear about what it is you desire. Then relentlessly pursue it. The path may have to change along the way, but that does not mean you stop going after exactly what you want.

10. Unequivocally, unapologetically, unconditionally love yourself: In the end, loving yourself alters everything. Every. Single. Thing. From how you see the day, to how you see yourself, to what you believe awaits you, to what you do with your one precious, beautiful life.

January 9

Life is filled with unanswered questions, but it is the courage to seek those
answers that continues to give meaning to life.
—J. D. Stroube

I decided it was time to sit down and ask my life a few questions.

Me: Where am I heading?
Life: To the place where you have clearly set your sights upon.

Me: When will I arrive?
Life: When you have learned the lessons placed before you.

Me: How am I to overcome my fears?
Life: You walk right through them. That is how.

Me: What if I am to fail?
Life: Tell me, what is to fail? I know not of such things.

Me: Why have you chosen such a difficult path for me?
Life: Why would you choose to look at this path as anything but beautiful?

Me: Who am I supposed to become?
Life: Dear sweet child, this was never about who you become but learning to love
who you have always been.

January 10

*Sometimes taking a leap of faith requires an imaginative mind that
can create the ending you are unable to see.*
—Shannon L. Alder

Doubt, the scars I bore
Inflicted by past stumbles
Reopened by new failings
And still I leapt

Fear, the chains I wore
A constant reminder
Of my previous falls
And still I leapt

I can't, the words I swore
The echo of my belief
The whisper in my head
And still I leapt

Uncertainty, the wall I stood before
Limited by what I already knew
Imprisoned by all I do not know
And still I leapt

I had no reason to believe
My history had been written
I am not meant to fly
And still I leapt.

January 11

Today is the only day in which we have any power.
—Steve Maraboli

Today, this shall be my pledge to myself.

Today, my excuses will not be greater than the plans I have for myself.

Today, my fears will not stand in the way of the dreams I have for myself.

Today, my cannot will not deter me from doing all that I can for myself.

Today, my weakness will be no match for the strength I have in myself.

Today, my doubts will not speak louder than the belief I have in myself.

Today, my past will not determine the future I want for myself.

Today, my decisions will reflect the love I have for myself.

January 12

The powerful play goes on and you may contribute a verse.
—Walt Whitman

If given but one word to speak
With all your might, "yes"
For in the willingness to try
You shall truly take flight

If only two words be spoken
From your truest place, "I'm sorry"
For in the act of forgiving
You shall truly be free

If allowed but three words
Allow your heart, "I love you"
For in the unconditional
You shall truly feel alive

If four words were uttered
Find the courage, "I will not quit"
For in the refusal to surrender
You shall grow ever stronger

With the gift of five words
Repeat daily, "You are so worth it"
For in this simple acceptance
You shall find your value

And as you wake this day
Pause before the mirror
Then gently speak your verse
So you may always know

"Yes, I'm sorry. I love you. I will not quit. You are so worth it."

January 13

Do it badly; do it slowly; do it fearfully; do it any way you have to, but do it.
—Steve Chandler

"This is impossible," you once said.

Then you found the strength to do it.

"I am broken," you once said.

Then you put yourself together again.

"I can't do this," you once said.

Then you learned to love again

"I am afraid," you once said.

Then you summoned your courage.

"I am so very lost," you once said.

Then you walked through the darkness.

"I no longer believe," you once said.

Then you called upon hope.

When your story is written, it will not contain the words you once said.

It shall be penned by what you then did.

January 14

Your perspective on life comes from the cage you were held captive in.
—Shannon L. Alder

I built my own prison. The foundation I laid was made of fears. Fears so deep, so cemented in my being, they supported every wall of my prison. Fear of not being enough, of rejection, of my own light, of the dreams I had. Fear of failing, of losing, of loving, of living.

The four walls I constructed were of blame and anger, pain and regret. They surrounded me. Defined me. Entombed me.

Blame and anger, two adjacent walls. Attached to one another, they went up quickly. For as I blamed others, it justified my anger. And the angrier I became, the easier it was to blame someone else for my behavior, my shortcomings, my failures, my lot in life.

Pain, the wall that resulted from the course of my action, the path of my life, for my blame and anger left hurt in their wake. Pain, the wall upon which I carved my story. For I needed others to know of my hurt. Pain, the wall I clung to. For if I refused to let go, it made being angry an acceptable response. And my walls were reinforced.

Regret, the final wall of my prison cell. So many bricks laid of my own hands. Shame the mortar bound them together. Came to regret my words, my losses, my actions, and my life. For there was a toll exacted for the other walls I erected.

But you may notice my prison is empty these days. No longer my home. No longer my tomb. The walls no longer intact, the foundation crumbling. And you may ask, "What keys set you free?"

Acceptance. The chisel that wore away the blame. I am solely responsible for my choices, my responses, and my life. I am the gatekeeper.

Peace. The gentle force that removed my anger. I am at peace with where my path has led me. I am at peace where my feet are.

Letting go. The undoing of my pain. I no longer need to cling to my heartache. I can let it go. I am going to be OK.

Forgiveness. The removal of my regret. I am only human. Mistakes are a part of growing and learning. I am able to forgive myself.

Faith. The hammer that finally crumbled my fear. Faith walks beside me. And I do not fear. Faith guides me. And I am no longer afraid. Faith speaks to me. And when I listen, I am freed.

January 15

Courage doesn't happen when you have all the answers. It happens when you are ready to face the questions you have been avoiding your whole life.
—Shannon L. Alder

Life asked a question of me.

Life: How do you think you arrived here?
Me: It must have been blind luck, for so many miles I doubted I would make it.
Life: To keep walking when one is unsure, this speaks of hope.

Life: How do you think you arrived here?
Me: It must have been fear, for so many steps taken when I was afraid.
Life: To keep walking when one is afraid, this speaks of courage.

Life: How do you think you arrived here?
Me: It must have been an accident, for so many times I did not know where I was going.
Life: To keep walking when one is lost, this speaks of faith.

Life: How do you think you arrived here?
Me: It must have been weakness, for so many days found me broken.
Life: To keep walking when one is shattered, this speaks of strength.

Then I asked a question of life.

Me: How do you think I go on from here?
Life: It must be as you arrived, with hope, courage, faith, and strength.

January 16

Can you imagine what I could do if I could do all I can?
—Jeff Rich

I could continue to wander surrounded by darkness.

Or I can become a source of light.

I could continue this free falling.

Or I can unfurl the wings I've been given.

I could continue to stare at my Everest.

Or I can set myself to scaling the mountain rising before me.

I could continue to exist in the safety of my own comfort.

Or I can dare to risk failing greatly.

I could continue to suffer at the hands of all I am unable to alter.

Or I can be an agent of change.

I could continue to be a victim of wounds I will not let heal.

Or I can accept the scars earned for living as a warrior.

I could sum up how the story of my life will be played out: I can.

Again this day, I shall softly yet surely whisper, "I can."

For therein lies my most powerful truth.

January 17

Courage is the discovery that you may not win, and trying when you know you can lose.
—Tom Krause

It takes courage to risk failing

It takes strength to overcome setbacks

It takes discipline to change a lifestyle

It takes trust to walk where you've never been

It takes commitment to reach a goal

It takes faith to continue when the road is long

It takes one step to move forward

It takes time to see the changes

It takes love to help yourself blossom

You have always had what it takes.

So take what you have, and do what it takes.

January 18

I have accepted fear as part of life—specifically the fear of change...I have gone ahead despite the pounding in the heart that says: turn back...
—Erica Jong

The voice in my head said, "Turn back."

And I replied, "I'm afraid...I'm not going that way." And so I went ahead.

The beating in my heart said, "Turn back."

And I replied, "I'm afraid...there's nothing for me there." And so I went ahead.

The reflection in the mirror said, "Turn back."

And I replied, "I'm afraid...I've already been there." And so I went ahead.

The sign ahead said, "Turn back."

And I replied, "I'm afraid...there is someplace new I must see." And so I went ahead.

I came to the edge of all I know and said, "I'm afraid..."

And yet I went ahead.

January 19

What we seek when we wander usually leads us back home.
—Gina Greenlee

Times I must wander alone
Along a path of my very own
Others may not understand
Everything my life has planned

Times I must wander alone
Unearthing each and every stone
Searching for what I may never see
All the missing parts of me

Times I must wander alone
This is when I've truly grown
Upon a path winding and long
This is how I become strong

Time I must wander alone
Collecting seeds I've sown
As I grow into who I am to be
All a part of becoming me

Times I must wander alone
Away from all I've ever known
Yet no matter how far I roam
My road always leads me home.

January 20

You never know what's around the corner. It could be everything. Or it could be nothing. You keep putting one foot in front of the other, and then one day you look back and you've climbed a mountain.
—Tom Hiddleston

When the darkness encroached,
Wanting to settle into the deepest parts of me,
I made my way through to the light.

When the doubt came creeping,
Causing me to question my steps,
I made my way toward the truths I knew.

When the fear showed up,
Seeking to imprison me,
I made my way beyond those walls.

When the confusion seemed all around,
Bringing but questions,
I made my way to the answers only I understood.

When the heartache arrived,
Shattering the footpath my life was following,
I made my way along a new trail.

When you ask me how I made it,
I shall simply say, "I put one foot in front of the other."

January 21

Embrace relational uncertainty. It's called romance. Embrace spiritual uncertainty.
It's called mystery. Embrace occupational uncertainty. It's called destiny.
Embrace emotional uncertainty. It's called joy. Embrace intellectual
uncertainty. It's called revelation.
—Mark Batterson

I don't always know where I'm going, yet I know it is where I am meant to be. Faith.

I don't always know when I will arrive, yet I know I will get there. Trust.

I don't always know how I will make it, yet I know I will not fear failing. Courage.

I don't always know which path I should take, yet I know I will be all right. Hope.

I don't always know why I must walk these miles, yet I know I will find my answers. Growth.

I don't always know who I am becoming, yet I know I will believe in me. Worth.

I don't always know what life has in store for me, yet I know I will allow my heart to remain open to it. Love.

I don't always know. Yet somehow I know.

January 22

Effort only fully releases its reward after a person refuses to quit.
—Napoleon Hill

I have struggled. Often. For the journey has been difficult, demanding much of me.

I have felt pain. Often self-inflicted. For choosing to walk upon the thorn-littered path many would not dare venture upon.

I have fallen. Often not knowing if I would rise again. For the burdens I carry conspired with gravity to hold me down.

I have rested. Often the weariness sets in. For the warrior, battles can seem so endless.

I have had my moments of doubt. Often questioning my own dreams. For they feel at times impossible.

I have stopped to catch my breath. Often for fear of the breathlessness. For forgetting the moments I cannot breathe are not about dying but about truly living.

I have never quit. Often this is all that really matters.

January 23

He that is good for making excuses is seldom good for anything else.
—Benjamin Franklin

I have my excuses.

They are ever present.

Quietly waiting to be accepted, invited, worn.

I have my excuses.

They are never in short supply.

Seemingly they multiply if given air to breathe.

I have my excuses.

They appear real.

Their very presence often validates them.

I have my excuses.

But when I refuse to use them,

I never have to apologize for something I did not do.

January 24

The most powerful agent of change is a change of heart.
—B. J. Marshal

As you look at me
So much that I hide
You may never see
How I'm changing inside

It may not be shown
Not yet shining through
How much I've grown
A me you never knew

Not a picture others painted
Now too large for their frame
My image no longer tainted
Never more to wear that shame

So how did change begin?
Accepted who I am not
Found comfort in my skin
Grateful for all I've got

I may not seem like much
Be not fooled by what you see
Wrinkles, scars, and such
What matters is inside of me

A heart of a champion
The soul of a hero
A warrior who fought and won
The me I came to know.

January 25

Never look directly at the sun. Instead, look at the sunflower.
—Vera Nazarian

If you only see my weakness
You will never know my strength
For I stood again today
Despite the broken pieces

If you only see my limits
You will never know my journey
For I have come so far
Just to stand in this place

If you only see my trembling
You will never know my courage
For I leapt into the abyss
Not knowing if a net existed

If you only see my stumbles
You will never know my grace
For I have learned to dance
Carrying a broken heart

If you only see my scars
You will never know my beauty
For hidden deep within
A heart woven back together

If you only see my darkness
You will never know my light
For I found my way home
Simply holding on to hope.

January 26

Strength does not come from physical capacity. It comes from an indomitable will.
—Mahatma Gandhi

When you fall down
But stand back up
Strength

When you have excuses
But do not use them
Strength

When you are in pain
But choose not to suffer
Strength

When you are bone weary
But carry on
Strength

When you do not want to
But you do
Strength

When your heart is not in it
But still you dance
Strength

When you want to quit
But you don't
Strength

Strength. It is in the doing.

January 27

*It is not what they take away from you that counts. It's what you do
with what you have left.*
—Hubert H. Humphrey

I once counted my tears

And knew how many sorrows I had suffered.

I once counted my heartaches

And knew how many times I had been broken.

I once counted my losses

And knew how much I did not have.

I began to count the number of times I said "thank you" in my day

And learned how much I have to be grateful for.

I began to count my blessings

And learned how much I have always had.

I began to count the times I have hit my knees

And learned how many prayers have been received.

It is not that we count but what we count that counts.

January 28

I want my life to be my greatest story. My very existence will be
the greatest poem.
—Charlotte Eriksson

My story was one of darkness

Until I wrote, "I am a light."

My story was one of helplessness

Until I wrote, "I am powerful."

My story was one of regret

Until I wrote, "I am sorry."

My story was one of wandering

Until I wrote, "I am home."

My story was one of suffering

Until I wrote, "I am OK."

My story was one of fear

Until I wrote, "I am brave."

My story was one of doubt

Until I wrote, "I am worthy."

My story. It changed when I realized I am the author.

January 29

I may not be there yet, but I'm closer than I was yesterday.
—Jose N. Harris

I asked, "Am I there yet?"
Came the whisper, "No, the road is long."

I asked, "Why must I travel so far?"
Came the whisper, "There is much to learn along the way."

I asked, "Is there another way?"
Came the whisper, "This alone is your path."

I asked, "Is there a shortcut?"
Came the whisper, "It will not lead you where you must go."

I asked, "Does the path get easier?"
Came the whisper, "No, but you will get stronger."

I asked, "What if I fail?"
Came the whisper, "You will fail, perhaps often, and yet you must keep going."

Came the asking, "Will you still go?"
I whispered, "Yes."

January 30

*People spend their entire lives searching the world for the pieces that will
make them whole, yet those pieces are only found within them.*
—Ken Poirot

I have been searching all my life. For what, I am not always certain. I cannot often
put words to it.

Yet there is this undeniable ache in my soul. A constant yearning. Perhaps a haunting
would more clearly describe it, for I am terrified I shall never find it.

Maybe I have been searching for home. A place where they speak my language.
Another voice that whispers of passions and hopes and dreams. Too often I feel a
stranger in a strange land. For no one seems to understand me.

Maybe I have been searching for purpose. An understanding of why I am here and
what I am to do with this one finite, fragile existence. And in the end, will it have
mattered? For nothing I accomplish shall touch eternity.

Maybe I have been searching for growth. How I ache to simply be and to simply do
better in all phases of my life. For seldom have I found comfort in the status quo.

Maybe I have been searching for love. A love that simply whispers, "Welcome home."
A love that lets me know I have made a difference simply by being me. A love that
allows me to simply unfurl my wings and become all I was ever meant to be.

January 31

What may look like a small act of courage is courage nevertheless. The important thing is to be willing to take a step forward.
—Dr. Daisaku Ikeda

Something calls to me
Beyond my comfort zone
I go forth fearlessly
I am carved from stone

Where once I wouldn't tread
This very path I now own
And all that lies ahead
I am carved from stone

Build a bridge or wall
The choice is mine alone
No longer fearful of the fall
I am carved from stone

I shall reach my destination
Even if weary to the bone
I will continue to run
I am carved from stone

Just a castle in the sky
Or a dream overblown?
I have the courage to try
I am carved from stone.

February 1

Faith is to believe what you do not yet see; the reward for this faith is to see what you believe.
—Saint Augustine

I believe a single candle can light the deepest night.

I believe in the goodness of the human heart.

I believe hope is the strongest lifeline.

I believe kindness matters.

I believe in the power of prayer.

I believe love is eternal.

I believe life is beautiful.

I believe dreams and miracles happen.

I simply still believe.

February 2

This is the art of courage: to see things as they are and still believe that
the victory lies not with those who avoid the bad, but those who taste,
in living awareness, every drop of the good.
—Victoria Lincoln

I am unaware of where this day shall lead me,

And yet I walk unafraid.

For I hold hope and grace as my closest companions,

And they shall not lead me astray.

I am unaware of what this day shall bring me,

And yet I go forth with open arms.

For I hold gratitude and peace in my heart,

And they shall allow me to accept come what may.

I am unaware of when this day shall test me,

And yet I do not fear failure.

For I hold strength and courage as truths in my story,

And they shall not fail me.

Although I know not of this day, I am aware of who I am,

And this shall see me through.

February 3

I believe that when you realize who you really are, you understand
that nothing can stop you from becoming that person.
—Christine Lincoln

I am not the swiftest
Not first to the finish line
Yet I've never been defeated
Not once have I given up

I am not the most skilled
Just an ordinary human
Yet within me exists a miracle
An unquenchable desire

I am not the bravest
Riddled with doubt and fear
Yet they are not roadblocks
Mere mile markers now behind me

I am not the strongest
Been weathered and cracked
Yet at my weakest point
I refused to be broken

All that which I am not
Neither defines nor limits me
For I have known all along
They were simply my excuses

And when it ceases to be
About what I cannot do
About who I am not
I can become who I am.

February 4

I am not a broken heart, and I am not your fault.
—Charlotte Eriksson

When I stopped worrying about all that I am not, I found myself in all that I am.

I am not artistic. I am simply splashing all the colors on the canvas of my life.

I am not poetic. I am simply writing the verses of my heart.

I am not talented. I am simply understanding of my gifts.

I am not graceful. I am simply moving to the unique rhythm of my song.

I am not without fears. I am simply unwilling to be consumed by my doubts.

I am not perfect. I am simply at peace knowing 'twas never the expectation.

I am not a superhero. I am simply an ordinary human aware of his own power.

I am not amazing. I am simply unafraid to occasionally amaze myself.

I am not unbroken. I am simply put together with the best pieces of me.

I am not an inspiration. I am simply choosing to be inspired by the light, love, and wonder that surrounds me.

February 5

The question is not what you look at, but what you see.
—Henry David Thoreau

I am fragile when I look at my weakness.

I am strength when I look at all I have overcome.

I am lost when I look behind me.

I am on the right path when I look at the step ahead of me.

I am afraid when I look at all I have never done.

I am courage when I look at all that is possible.

I am filled with regret when I look at all I have lost.

I am filled with gratitude when I look at all I have.

I am awkward when I look at the dance of another.

I am grace when I look at the ballet of my life.

I am a scarred and aging fighter when I look at my reflection.

I am a beautiful warrior when I look at my heart.

I am what I choose to look at.

February 6

I think this is what we all want to hear: that we are not alone in hitting the bottom, and that it is possible to come out of that place courageous, beautiful, and strong.
—Anna White

Along the way, I may stumble
And you shall offer your hand
I may not ever reach for it
Knowing you care, I shall rise

Along the way, I may falter
And you shall slow your pace
I may wave you to move along
Knowing you're out there, I will go on

Along the way, I may become lost
And you shall want to be a compass
I may not look to you for direction
Knowing you left a trail, I will find my way

Along the way, I may be frightened
And you shall try to calm my fears
I may never be as brave as you
Knowing you had the courage, I will overcome

Along the way, we may become separated
And you shall wonder where I am
I may not arrive where you now stand
Knowing you, I know I never walk alone.

February 7

When you understand, that what you're telling is just a story. It isn't happening anymore. When you realize the story you're telling is just words, when you can just crumble up and throw your past in the trashcan, then we'll figure out who you're going to be.
—Chuck Palahniuk

I read between the lines of your story.

Where you wrote, "I am so afraid,"
I read, "Now I must summon my courage."

Where you wrote, "I got knocked down,"
I read, "Now I must become a fighter."

Where you wrote, "I am so very lost,"
I read, "Now I must find my way."

Where you wrote, "I cannot go on,"
I read, "Now I must take one more step."

Where you wrote, "I no longer believe,"
I read, "Now I must call on faith."

Where you wrote, "I am broken,"
I read, "Now I must pick up the pieces."

I read between the lines of your story, and, there, I found your truth.

For the chapters written were merely preludes to what you chose to do.

And, there, your life's story is told.

February 8

You will never get everything in life but you will get enough.
—Sanhita Baruah

This is my wish for you: enough

Strength enough to stand once more

Faith enough to pray once more

Courage enough to risk once more

Grace enough to forgive once more

Trust enough to believe once more

Hope enough to try once more

Happiness enough to smile once more

Love enough to give once more.

I wish for you: enough.

February 9

There are questions that are not meant to be answered with words. Some questions take a lifetime to answer. Take action.
—J. R. Rim

I have always questioned my life.

It is a part of my search for meaning, for purpose, for direction, for an understanding of what I am supposed to do.

Once again, I had questions. Once more, life had answers. That conversation went something like this:

Me: How do I know which direction I am to go?
Life: There can be only one direction: forward.

Me: What happens if I should fail?
Life: There can be only one response: you try again.

Me: When will I reach the finish line?
Life: There can be only one time: when you decide to stop.

Me: Where will this road lead me?
Life: There can be only one place: exactly where you are supposed to be.

Me: Why then am I so often taken to the ledge?
Life: There can be only one reason: you are meant to fly.

And should I listen to the answers of my life, my list of things to do each and every day becomes simple and clear:

1. Move forward
2. Try again
3. Don't quit
4. Find comfort where you stand
5. Launch yourself

February 10

I have not always chosen the safest path. I've made my mistakes, plenty of them. I sometimes jump too soon and fail to appreciate the consequences. But I've learned something important along the way: I've learned to heed the call of my heart. I've learned that the safest path is not always the best path and I've learned that the voice of fear is not always to be trusted.
—Steve Goodier

Somewhere along the way, I got lost.

For the detours and dead ends.

Somewhere along the way, I got lost.

For the missteps and U-turns.

Somewhere along the way, I got lost.

For the roads taken and those not traveled.

Somewhere along the way, I got lost.

For looking back and losing sight of what lies ahead.

Somewhere along the way, I got lost.

For the lack of direction and lack of trust.

Somewhere along the way, I got lost.

But I shall find my way home. For my heart knows which way to go.

And from this day forth, it shall be my compass.

February 11

Don't ever give up. Don't ever give in. Don't ever stop trying. Don't ever sell out.
And if you find yourself succumbing to one of the above for a brief moment, pick
yourself up, brush yourself off, whisper a prayer, and start where you left off.
But never, ever, ever give up.
—Richelle E. Goodrich

Do not count the number of times I have fallen.

Count instead the times I rose to my feet after being down.

This is the measure of me.

Do not count the number of times I have failed.

Count instead the times I willed myself to try again.

This is the measure of me.

Do not count the number of times I have wanted to give up.

Count instead the times I continued on.

This is the measure of me.

Do not count the number of times I have hesitated out of fear.

Count instead the times I leapt despite being afraid.

This is the measure of me.

Do not count the number of times I have been broken.

Count instead the times I picked up the pieces and stitched myself back together.

This is the measure of me.

February 12

Worry is a misuse of the imagination.
—Dan Zadra

Each day, I hold fast to the simple adage "Trust more, worry less."

Where there is pain, I trust I will find healing.

Where there is disappointment, I trust I will learn gratitude in that moment.

Where there is fear, I trust I will know a courage that cannot be shaken.

Where there are obstacles, I trust I will summon the strength to move beyond them.

Where there is the voice of doubt, I trust I will hear the whisper of faith.

Where there is brokenness, I trust I will dig deep enough to find the parts of me that remain whole.

Where there is worry, I simply trust more.

February 13

Physical strength can never permanently withstand the impact of spiritual force.
—Eleanor Roosevelt

It is not my strength that gives me wings.

It is a spirit longing to soar.

It is not my strength that guides my way.

It is a spirit leading me home.

It is not my strength that compels me forward.

It is a spirit constantly seeking higher ground.

It is not my strength that carries me beyond the obstacles.

It is a spirit refusing to bow.

It is not my strength. It is the force of my spirit.

And it is a force to be reckoned with.

February 14

Love is patient, love is kind. It does not envy, it does not boast, it is not proud. It is not rude, it is not self-seeking, it is not easily angered, it keeps no record of wrongs. Love does not delight in evil but rejoices with the truth. It always protects, always trusts, always hopes, always perseveres.
—1 Corinthians 13: 4–8

May you know a love of self

For it shall set you free

May you know a love of family

For it shall welcome you home

May you know a love of friends

For it shall bring you comfort

May you know the love of strangers

For it shall renew your faith

May you know a love of today

For it shall bring hope for your tomorrows

May you know a love of tomorrow

For it shall hold your dreams

Today and always, I hope you know love.

February 15

Define yourself; you have the monopoly on your life's dictionary.
—Matshona Dhliwayo

You cannot simply be measured by a number.

Not on a scale.

It cannot measure your strength or courage.

Not on a clock.

It cannot count your blessings or triumphs.

Not on a piece of paper.

It cannot mark how far you have come.

Not on a calendar.

It cannot tell the story of how much you have grown.

You are so much more than a number.

February 16

*As my sufferings mounted I soon realized that there were two ways
in which I could respond to my situation—either to react with bitterness or
seek to transform the suffering into a creative force. I decided to follow
the latter course.*
—Martin Luther King Jr.

Should you tell me you are hurting, I shall ask if you want to heal.

Should you tell me you are afraid, I shall ask if you will show me your courage.

Should you tell me you are defeated, I shall ask if you can continue to fight.

Should you tell me you are giving up, I shall ask if it is worth it for you to try once more.

Should you tell me you have fallen, I shall ask if you arose.

And then I shall wait to hear you answer, "Yes."

February 17

*We all have dreams. But in order to make dreams come into reality, it takes
an awful lot of determination, dedication, self-discipline, and effort.*
—Jesse Owens

A dream is not built out of doubts.

It is built from hopes.

A dream is not constructed from intentions.

It is constructed through actions.

A dream is not achieved by having excuses.

It is achieved by keeping promises.

A dream is not reached by fearing what you think you cannot do.

It is reached by believing in your possibilities.

February 18

But this is how some get lost in the race of life, they spend their lives judging how much they will do or how much they should do based on what everyone else around them is doing.
—Stephen Richards

We are not moving at the same pace. And it is OK.

For we shall all arrive in our own time.

We are not traveling the same road. And it is OK.

For we are all heading in the right direction.

We are not running the same race. And it is OK.

For we are all seeking a finish line.

We are not going to end up in the same place. And it is OK.

For we are all going to be where we are meant to be.

We are not chasing the same dream. And it is OK.

For we are all believing in our possibilities.

We are not fighting the same battle. And it is OK.

For we are all warriors.

February 19

Either I will find a way, or I will make one.
—Philip Sydney

I will not fear the darkness.

I will be a source of light.

I will not question the journey.

I will trust my steps.

I will not doubt the course.

I will steer the vessel.

I will not look back.

I will keep focused on where I am going.

I will not run from my past.

I will stand and embrace the present.

I will not give in to the regret.

I will celebrate the blessings in my life.

I will not listen to the whisper of "I can't."

I will shout from the mountains, "I can."

February 20

The will to win, the desire to succeed, the urge to reach your full potential...
these are the keys that will unlock the door to personal excellence.
—Confucius

There are questions seeking answers of me.
It is not that I know what I will find.
It is simply that I am unafraid of my truth.

There are challenges rising before me.
It is not that I am strong or brave enough to face them.
It is simply that I have no other choice.

There are fears that walk right beside me.
It is not that I am never afraid.
It is simply that I shall not bow to them.

There is a place I must go to.
It is not that I know exactly where I am headed.
It is that I simply cannot afford to remain here.

There are many miles ahead of me.
It is not that I should or have to go.
It is simply that I will.

February 21

I can't change the direction of the wind, but I can adjust
my sails to always reach my destination.
—Jimmy Dean

I cannot condemn my circumstances, for often, they were created by my hand.
But I can work to change them.

I cannot rewind to a distant past, for what is done is done.
But I can move gracefully forward to a new future.

I cannot forget that which has left these scars, for they are a part of me.
But I can forgive so they no longer hold power over me.

I cannot state that I shall no longer fear, for much frightens me.
But I can trust I will again find the courage.

I cannot guarantee I shall never fall, for I have my frailties.
But I can promise to rise every time I stumble.

February 22

Men who fear demons see demons everywhere.
—Brom

We all have our "it,"

That something that sits in front of us. Impeding our progress. Limiting our growth. Casting a shadow on our path.

For some, "it" is as close as the next breath. And it is here. For some, "it" is on the distant horizon simply awaiting our inevitable arrival. And it is there.

For some, "it" is as real as the rising sun. It will be there when the morn again breaks. For some, "it" is as imaginary as the monsters conjured up under the bed. It will be there when darkness again falls.

Near or far. Real or imagined. The truth is we must find a way to move beyond whatever "it" is. But how?

First, clearly identify what "it" is. Is it your past, your ghost, your fear, your excuses, your crutch, your impossible, your Everest, your own self?

Second, be accepting of the fact that "it" is there. You cannot deny it or hide it or pretend it does not exist. Own its presence in your life.

Next, recognize why "it" is there. Is there a lesson you must take from it? Is there work you must do with it? What does it want from you or you from it?

Then whether you have a plan or not and whether you are ready or not, you must find a way to the other side. It has to be put behind you.

Face it. Do battle with it. Deconstruct it one brick at a time. Run through it. Go around it. Climb over it. Blow the thing up.

Do what you have to do. But for your own good, stop standing there, staring at "it."

Finally, be done with "it." It is behind you. Or in ruins. Or no more a part of you. Or no longer serving your good.

I wish for you to be on the other side of "it." For therein awaits freedom, peace, joy, love, life.

February 23

The two hardest tests on the spiritual road are the patience to wait for the right moment and the courage not to be disappointed with what we encounter.
—Paulo Coelho

With urgency comes a need.

Where need exists, there is a void from believing you do not have enough.

With patience comes acceptance.

Where acceptance exists, there is gratitude for knowing you have all you need.

With urgency comes chaos.

Where chaos exists, there is panic from believing only in the now.

With patience comes peace.

Where peace exists, there is serenity for understanding the power of yet.

With urgency come limits.

Where limits exist, there is confinement for never allowing yourself to grow.

With patience comes freedom.

Where freedom exists, there is flight for allowing your wings to develop.

Patience, my dear friend. Patience.

February 24

Humanity does not suffer from the disease of wrong beliefs but humanity suffers from the contagious nature of the lack of belief. If you have no magic with you it is not because magic does not exist but it is because you do not believe in it. Even if the sun shines brightly upon your skin every day, if you do not believe in the sunlight, the sunlight for you does not exist.
—C. JoyBell C.

When I believe I have nothing left to hold on to
I can always cling to hope

When I believe I have nothing left to count on
I can always place my hand on my beating heart

When I believe I have nothing left to change
I can always grow to change what I believe

When I believe I have nothing left to give
I can always offer my forgiveness

When I believe I have nothing left to say
I can always say a prayer

When I believe I have nothing left to believe in
I can always believe in me.

February 25

When you find your path, you must not be afraid. You need to have sufficient courage to make mistakes. Disappointment, defeat, and despair are the tools God uses to show us the way.
—Paulo Coelho

At times I do not feel so strong
Days I simply stumble along
Times I am not so brave
The world I am unable to save
Lost on the way to becoming
Known a pain so numbing
From my tears there was no hiding
For the hurt deep and abiding

Wish that I could disappear
Be anywhere but here
Days come the sadness
A world full of madness
Mistakes I have made my share
Do I try again, do I dare?
Try to be perfect but fail
Broken dreams litter the trail

But today again I will rise
Still so many chances, so many tries
And with much good intent
Myself I hope to reinvent
Be simply better than I was
Make mistakes just because
I am simply human, that is all
I will be OK should I fall

Rise again, check for any broken part
Knowing deep down in my heart
I am free to make a mistake
It is just a chance I dare to take
Dare to try something new
Do not fear being you
In your mistakes and frailty
You come to see your true beauty.

February 26

What you're missing is that the path itself changes you.
—Julien Smith

Dear Life,

Just in case you didn't know
Something in me changed today
This is not how the story will go
No more shall I live this way

Been frightened by many things
Chained and unable to fly
As if someone clipped my wings
Was just my unwillingness to try

Of my life I am now captain
No more sitting on the sideline
I've waited so long to begin
It is my turn to finally shine

I started living instead of existing
No more shall I live in fear
Change no longer resisting
My path now suddenly clear

And so I am on my way
Ahead, so much to celebrate
Cannot wait another day
You are calling, and I can't be late.

Love, Me

February 27

With all its sham and drudgery, it is still a beautiful world.
—Max Ehrmann

I've seen the shadows
As they enveloped me
Yet my spirit knows
A light that shines brightly

I've seen the breaking
Been on bended knees
New steps I'm taking
For courage heard the pleas

I've seen the beast in me
Wanted to avert my stare
Looking closer, I can see
The beauty within there

I've seen my life undone
So much stripped away
With the rising of a new sun
I know that I will be OK

I've seen love walk away
Through tear-filled eyes
'Twas never meant to stay
For love needs no alibis

Seen the best and the worst
As life has been unfurled
Been blessed and cursed
But still it's a beautiful world.

February 28

Two things define you, your attitude when you are at your
worst and your attitude when you are at your best.
—Tanya Masse

Believing what I am unable to yet see: hope

Trusting what I know not yet: faith

Letting go when darkness keeps the net invisible: courage

Moving forward when obstacles block the path: perseverance

Forgiving what has broken me: humanity

Giving when nothing is expected in return: love

May these define my life.

March 1

We are products of our past, but we don't have to be prisoners of it.
—Rick Warren

My past tells a story
One of where I've been
I am not reading those words
I am busy writing a new chapter

My past sings a song
One recorded long ago
I am not singing those lyrics
I am finding a new voice

My past paints a picture
One in faded black and whites
I am not tied to that image
I am out chasing new rainbows

My past was a journey
One that led me somewhere
I am not obligated to remain there
I am seeking out a new path

March 2

Yesterday is gone. Tomorrow has not yet come. We have only today. Let us begin.
—*Mother Teresa*

No matter how far I have come
Today, I must start again
For I will not reach my destination
If I remain where yesterday found me

No matter how strong I have become
Today, I must start again
For I will not overcome tomorrow's battle
With the strength of yesterday

No matter how brave I appear
Today, I must start again
For I will not find the courage
Holding on to fears of yesterday

No matter how much I believe
Today, I must start again
For I will not see the light of hope
If yesterday's doubts cast their darkness

Today, I must start again.

March 3

It's daring to be curious about the unknown, to dream big dreams, to live outside prescribed boxes, to take risks, and above all, daring to investigate the way we live until we discover the deepest treasured purpose of why we are here.
—Luci Swindoll

I hope you dare

I hope you dare to choose failing greatly over failing to try

I hope you dare to taste your fears over tasting the bitterness of regret

I hope you dare to chase the impossible over settling for the comfort of your own limits

I hope you dare to spread your wings over standing at the edge

I hope you dare to break yourself wide open over fearing your brokenness

I hope you dare to be your own superhero over hoping to be rescued.

March 4

Life is not made up of minutes, hours, days, weeks, months, or years, but of
moments. You must experience each one before you can appreciate it.
—Sarah Ban Breathnach

Life is but a finite set of moments.
And within those moments, we decide how we shall live.

There comes a moment you will have to face your fears or turn and run.
Face your fears.

There comes a moment you will have to believe you can or doubt you will.
Believe you can.

There comes a moment you will tell yourself, "Take a chance" or "Not a chance."
Take the chance.

There comes a moment you will celebrate that you tried or regret that you never did.
Celebrate.

There comes a moment you will have to decide: jump or stand still.
Jump.

Life is but a finite set of moments. Live each one.

March 5

You can run away from yourself so often, and so much, just because the broken
pieces of you cut your feet too deeply if you stay around for too long. But then what
if someone were to come along and pick up those pieces for you? Then you wouldn't
have to run away from yourself anymore. You could stop running. If someone
sees you as something worth staying with—maybe you'll stay with yourself, too.
—C. JoyBell C.

I ran, trying to outrun the heartbreak.
And yet it chased me down.

I ran, trying to hide from the pain.
And yet it found me lost.

I ran, trying to rid myself of sorrow.
And yet it overtook all of me.

I ran, trying to escape the feeling of inadequacy.
And yet it utterly consumed me.

I ran, trying to avoid the darkness.
And yet it swallowed me whole.

I ran, trying to dispel the fear.
And yet it still followed me.

I grew weary of the running. Had to finally face that which pursued me.
And yet, when I turned around, 'twas only my shadow.

No longer will I run from me.

March 6

A very small percentage of the people in this world will actually experience and live today. So many people will be stuck on another day, another time that traumatized them and caused them to spiritually stutter so they miss out on this day.
—Steve Maraboli

The time to take a chance
To go ahead and dance
Letting joy come your way
It feels like today

The moment to let go of fear
When you will say, "I'm here"
Fear no longer in the way
It feels like today

When you will finally let go
Of what you think you know
In the past not meant to stay
It feels like today

Nevermore to simply wait
Nor continue to hesitate
A new chapter in your play
It feels like today

Best prepare for tomorrow
Time we can never borrow
Don't let dreams slip away

March 7

Everybody knows that. The missing step is always the next.
—Oscar Lopes

Stood before my mountain
Yet another one to climb
Asked how shall I get this done
A single step at a time

But this mountain is new
Above me it does soar
It remains this way through
One step then one step more

Of the climb I grow weary
This summit may not reach
Take a step, you will see
You draw closer with each

The mountain is my destiny
To climb my life's writ
One single step sets me free
In this step, my refusal to quit.

March 8

To believe in something, and not to live it, is dishonest.
—Mahatma Gandhi

I believe in hope and light
Doing good and living right
In love and laughter
And happily ever after

I believe in tomorrow
That faith trumps sorrow
In the gift of giving
And simply living

I believe in the mystery
That which I cannot see
In one more try
And my ability to fly

I believe in the dance
Daring to take a chance
In trusting the leap
And promises I must keep

Life is what we believe in.

March 9

I'm not asking you to walk in my shoes; I'd never wish my afflictions on anyone.
But could you walk beside me on secure ground and reach to hold my hand?
—Richelle E. Goodrich

If I could walk your path for you, I would pass.
For there are lessons for you to learn along the way.

But I will want to know all you have learned.

If I could remove obstacles from your path, I would not.
For there you shall find your strength.

But I will offer my hand should you stumble.

If I could change the path you are on, I would refuse.
For this is the way you must go.

But I will be there when you arrive where you are going.

If I could travel with you as you go, I would surely rejoice.
For I shall be witness to your growth, your strength, your coming home.

My challenge was never to save you from your path.
For this you did not ask.

But should you ask, "Walk with me?"
I shall gently take your hand and quietly say, "I can."

March 10

This life is yours. Take the power to choose what you want to do and do it well.
Take the power to love what you want in life and love it honestly. Take the power
to walk in the forest and be a part of nature. Take the power to control your
own life. No one else can do it for you. Take the power to make your life happy.
—Susan Polis Schutz

Fear screams
Hope whispers
Listen to the quiet

Weakness is superficial
Strength lies buried
Dig deep

Doubt can paralyze
Belief can free
Learn to trust

Regret is a thief
Forgiveness is a gift
Accept the present

Cannot limits
Can expands
Pick one

For every negative
There exists a positive
And we always have a choice

The power lies with you.

March 11

Give up trying to make me give up.
—Masashi Kishimoto

I think you should give up.

Give up doubting what you know is your truth.

Give up believing your limits of yesterday.

Give up discounting your achievements.

Give up questioning your strength.

Give up downplaying your gifts.

Give up fearing your light.

Give up accepting less than your worth.

Give up giving up.

March 12

Endurance precedes success.
—Wayne Chirisa

When so very sore
I shall find some way
Pick myself up off the floor
Get on with the day

When nothing left but weak
I shall call on my strong
No excuses will I speak
Just keep moving along

When filled with tired
I shall rise above it
In my pity not stay mired
There can be no quit

When riddled with doubt
I shall still get it done
Life always figures it out
Answers to every question

When standing on the ledge
I shall simply take the leap
Past my comfort's edge
Many promises to keep

When feeling defeated
I shall continue to endure
My history will be repeated
For there exists a warrior

When challenges arise
I shall refuse to bow
Eyes kept on the prize
A dream approaches now.

March 13

Dance. Smile. Giggle. Marvel. Trust. Hope. Love. Wish. Believe. Most of all, enjoy every moment of the journey, and appreciate where you are at this moment instead of always focusing on how far you have to go.
—Mandy Hale

If you can notice less the scars of your weakness

You will better see the beauty of your strength

If you can nevermore announce yourself by your failures

All you have dared try shall speak loudly for you

If you can break up with the excuses that once held you down

You will fall in love with the feeling of flying free

If you resist measuring yourself by the number of times you have fallen

You shall begin to realize you have always risen to your feet

If you can focus not solely on how far you have yet to go

You will stand in awe of just how far you have already traveled.

March 14

Do you want me to tell you something really subversive? Love is everything
it's cracked up to be. That's why people are so cynical about it. It really
is worth fighting for, being brave for, risking everything for. And the trouble
is, if you don't risk anything, you risk even more.
—Erica Jong

To keep digging when the well appears dry
This is to know faith.

To forgive when the wrong appears unforgivable
This is to know peace.

To walk on when the path appears dark
This is to know courage

To continue when the giving up appears inevitable
This is to know growth

To climb when the mountain appears insurmountable
This is to know hope

To rise when the burden appears too great
This is to know strength

To risk again when the heart appears broken
This is to know love

March 15

I love you without knowing how, or when, or from where. I love you simply,
without problems or pride: I love you in this way because I do not know any other
way of loving but this, in which there is no I or you, so intimate that your hand
upon my chest is my hand, so intimate that when I fall asleep your eyes close.
—*Pablo Neruda*

The burdens we bear may not be the same. Yet I shall not add to the weight as you carry on.

The scars we have earned may not be the same. Yet I shall not discount your pain as you attempt to heal.

The truths we hold in our hearts may not be the same. Yet I shall simply listen as you speak yours.

The paths we walk may not be the same. Yet I shall not impede your journey as you travel along.

The dreams we dream may not be the same. Yet I shall celebrate you as you reach for yours.

The lives we live may not be the same. Yet I shall wish for you joy as you get on with the business of living.

The love we seek may not be the same. Yet I shall hope you find the greatest of loves as you search for home.

You and I are not the same. Yet I shall treat you as though we are one and the same, for this is to love.

March 16

We teach best by how we live life; who we are instructs with absolute clarity.
—Bryant McGill

"Fill in the bubble completely. Make your mark heavy and dark."

Simple instructions. On every fill-in-the-bubble test I have ever given or taken.

Simple instructions. For how life is truly meant to be lived.

And yet how many of us are willing to live in such a way as to make our mark?

It seems we so rarely "fill in the bubble." For fear of straying outside the lines. For believing rules that were never meant to be followed. And so we contain ourselves. We leave empty spaces. We let dreams go unfulfilled.

It seems we so rarely "make our mark."
For fear of pushing too hard. For believing the choices we make for ourselves are incorrect. And so we doubt. We hesitate. We come to fear our own answers.

And in doing so, we fail to remember that this test called life came complete with a simple set of instructions. We simply need follow them.

Fill in the bubble completely. Make your mark heavy and dark.

March 17

It takes strength and courage to admit the truth.
—Rick Riordan

I remember driving along a desolate stretch of county highway. The night was still. The hour was late. Or early, depending on how you viewed it.

I was far from where I had been yet not sure where I was headed. I suspect this is what is meant by being in the middle of nowhere.

We sat in silence, the driver and I. Only the miles hummed along. We sat in the darkness. Our faces illuminated only by the dashboard lights.

The driver wanted to know my story. Of how I came to be where I was. And there, as if making my confessional, I shared my brokenness.

I spoke of my most recent failure and how I was told I would "never amount to anything."

These words did not serve as fuel to a fire. But as a blanket that smothered the flame.

These words did not serve as a spark to light my path. But as a fog that plunged me further into the darkness.

These words became my prophecy, for with each failure, it only further validated that I would "never amount to anything."

The driver listened intently as I finished. And once again, the silence came upon us. Only the miles hummed along.

As we drew closer to our destination, the driver finally spoke, and this is all she said: "Did it ever occur to you that they were wrong?"

And in that moment, in that single simple question, the fog was lifted. For never once had I considered that.

I had simply accepted those words as truth. As if the mere utterance of those words now made them an undeniable fact.

Since then I have not lived in hope of somehow proving those words wrong.

I have lived in such a way as to never allow another to ever speak my truth.

March 18

There are beautiful things in the world and there are sad things and when they come together they make a star. The light is far away and the strangest part is that the light is inside you.
—Victor Lodato

Perhaps strength is not something you must acquire.

Maybe it simply exists within you and waits for a time when you must be strong.

Perhaps courage is not something you must acquire.

Maybe it sits quietly within you and waits for a time when you must be brave.

Perhaps faith is not something you must acquire.

Maybe it breathes softly within you and waits for a time when you must believe.

Perhaps worthiness is not something you must acquire.

Maybe it waits patiently within you until a time when you recognize your true value.

Perhaps you would view yourself differently if you no longer believed you are deficient.

Maybe the time has come for you to recognize that you have always been enough.

For what you seek has always been within.

March 19

Maybe "okay" will be our "always"...
—John Green

It is OK to have questions.

It is how you discover your answers.

It is OK to experience doubt.

It is how you discover your faith.

It is OK to give in to the brokenness.

It is how you discover your wholeness.

It is OK to give over to the fear.

It is how you discover your courage.

It is OK to let your heart be exposed.

It is how you discover your truest loves.

It is OK to simply stand motionless.

It is how you discover your direction.

It is OK to fall due to weakness.

It is how you discover your strength to stand.

What you will discover is that it is going to be OK.

March 20

Scared is what you're feeling. Brave is what you're doing.
—Emma Donoghue

Do not fear the path that stretches out before you.

You have always found your way. And you will once again.

Do not fear the emptiness of going it alone.

You have always been enough. And this truth shall fill you up.

Do not fear the falls along the way.

You have always picked yourself back up. And this time shall be no different.

Do not fear the weariness settling in.

You have always had the strength to carry on. And you are stronger than you know.

Do not fear the impending ledge.

You have always had wings. And now you simply need to unfurl them.

Do not fear.

March 21

All my relationships and all of my challenges are opportunities for my soul to evolve.
—Eileen Anglin

Got knocked down
Battered and bruised
From there learned to crawl
Vowed to move forward

Grew weary of the crawling
Found strength to rise to my knees
Took a moment to pray
For courage to stand once again

Stood on uncertain ground
Not lost, yet not knowing
With each step, strength returned
Found courage to live again

This is my journey
This my evolution
So many truths yet to discover
Yet one already learned

I will not crawl again.

March 22

Take your life into your own hands, and what happens?
A terrible thing: no one to blame.
—Erica Jong

I stumbled
Only to realize it was over the laces these hands failed to tie.

I came upon a wall
Only to realize it was built by these hands.

I was broken into pieces
Only to realize it was these hands holding the hammer.

I encountered the darkness
Only to realize these hands held a light all along.

I was shackled
Only to realize these hands threw away the key.

I could not bear the story
Only to realize these hands penned every chapter.

I changed my life
Only when I realized the power held within these two hands.

March 23

If you aren't in over your head, how do you know how tall you are?
—T. S. Eliot

If I never jump into the deep end
Never leap into the unknown abyss
The fears I hold shall never end
So many chances do I miss

If I never get in over my head
Never dare go beyond my limit
The wall I know I come to dread
So many times that is where I quit

If I never push past the pain
Never embrace the searing heat
The place I stand is where I remain
So many ways comes defeat

If I never get knocked to the ground
Never learn to rise from the fall
The strength in me is never found
How then will I ever stand tall?

I will no longer fear going under
To break the surface I shall fight
Never more will I need to wonder
If I can reach a brand-new height.

March 24

In spite of discouragement and adversity, those who are happiest
seem to have a way of learning from difficult times, becoming
stronger, wiser and happier as a result.
—Joseph B. Wirthlin

I will be strong
And when pain comes
Driving me to my knees
I shall rise once more

I will be strong of faith
And when pain comes
Bringing with it doubt
I shall still believe

I will be strong of spirit
And when pain comes
Hoping to clip my wings
I shall still take flight

I will be strong of will
And when pain comes
Thinking it can stop me
I shall continue on

I will be strong of heart
And when pain comes
Hurting me most
I shall not be broken

I will be strong today
And come tomorrow
Should pain return
It shall find me stronger

March 25

Courage to me is doing something daring, no matter how afraid,
insecure, intimidated, alone, unworthy, incapable, ridiculed or whatever
other paralyzing emotion you might feel. Courage is taking action...
no matter what. So you're afraid? Be afraid. Be scared silly to the
point you're trembling and nauseous, but do it anyway!
—Richelle E. Goodrich

Wonder all I've missed
For the fear of going
Fruits I've never kissed
Afraid of not knowing

What treasure passed by
Much I did not receive
For being afraid to try
Because I did not believe

What paths did I not cross?
Walked but a narrow trail
A victory became a loss
As I was too afraid to fail

Sat out so many dances
For fear can paralyze
Afraid to take the chances
Fear speaks convincing lies

Fear's a hangman's rope
For dreams it can strangle
Fear's the thief of hope
An empty life left to dangle

Yet I long to finally dance
Despite fear in my heart
Decided to take a stance
Allowed the music to start

A treasure waits inside
Where once I feared to tread
No longer will I be denied
I choose courage instead

March 26

Luck has a way of evaporating when you lean on it.
—Brandon Mull

I know you face many challenges. And while I wish for you many things as you set out to face them, I will not wish for you luck.

I will not wish for you luck. I will wish for you faith.

For when you believe, that which you desire shall be realized.

I will not wish for you luck. I will wish for you trust.

For when you fully trust yourself, impossible is a lie.

I will not wish for you luck. I will wish for you strength.

For when you find your strength, the obstacles set before you shall disappear.

I will not wish for you luck. I will wish for you hope.

For when you have hope as your partner, there is always a light on the path.

I will not wish for you luck. I will wish for you peace.

For when you allow peace to reign, the worries you hold simply dissolve.

I will not wish for you luck. I will wish for you confidence.

For a quiet, steady confidence in yourself will lead you where you are meant to be.

I will not wish for you luck.

I will wish for you to know you already have everything you need to see you through.

March 27

Our decisions are the one thing we can control. Today's
the day to make those choices really count.
—Michael Hyatt

I am equipped to face this day.

Faith will guide me through the darkness

Hope will lift me from my knees

Trust will calm my trembling

Strength will ease my burden

Discipline will fuel my decisions

Courage will move me forward

Kindness will be my first choice

Patience will slow my harried pace

Gratitude will provide me perspective

Love will be my signature.

March 28

*The true measure of a person's character is how one
handles one's failures, not successes.*
—Bill Courtney

How do you measure courage?

By the number of times you jumped despite the fear.

How do you measure success?

By the number of times you tried again despite the desire to quit.

How do you measure strength?

By the number of times you got back up despite getting knocked down.

How do you measure the size of your heart?

By the number of times it beats despite the breaking.

How do you measure faith?

By the number of times you believed despite not knowing.

By any standard, you measure up.

March 29

The lesson is this: When the road gets dark and all hope
seems lost, there's nothing to do but keep going.
—Sarah Arthur

If you long to know how far you can go, you must keep moving

If you long to know much you can achieve, you must keep trying

If you long to know how many summits you can reach, you must keep climbing

If you long to know how brave you are, you must keep facing the fear

If you long to know how brilliant your light is, you must keep shining

If you long to know how great your faith is, you must keep believing

Thus, the greatest lesson of all: you simply must.

March 30

*Twenty years from now you will be more disappointed by the things that you
didn't do than by the ones you did do. So throw off the bowlines. Sail away from
the safe harbor. Catch the trade winds in your sails. Explore. Dream. Discover.*
—H. Jackson Brown Jr.

A dream is whispering your name
But you must listen above your own noise

A new path is unfolding before you
But you must look beyond your current circumstances

A promise is waiting for you to keep it
But you must rise to your level of excellence

A healing is asking for you to receive it
But you must answer yes in your heart

A prayer is waiting to be answered
But you must first take to your knees and whisper it

A day is coming for you to completely seize it
But you must live it with your arms wide open

March 31

*Owning our story can be hard but not nearly as difficult as spending our
lives running from it. Embracing our vulnerabilities is risky but not nearly
as dangerous as giving up on love and belonging and joy—the experiences
that make us the most vulnerable. Only when we are brave enough to
explore the darkness will we discover the infinite power of our light.*
—Brene Brown

Came the darkness
Wandered lost and alone
Afraid and helpless
Yet ahead a tiny light shone

Surrounded by shadows
As my heart was aching
Battered by life's blows
'Twas a dawn still breaking

Fell into the deepest hole
Until left with nothing
A lonely, barren soul
Above a light flickering

No matter how dark the night
A light did always shine
It must be kept in sight
Hope was the light of mine

The darkness cannot hide
Nor dim this lit candle
When hope is held inside
Whatever comes, you can handle.

I wish you light. I wish you hope.

April 1

Quitting is not giving up, it's choosing to focus your attention on something more important. Quitting is not losing confidence, it's realizing that there are more valuable ways you can spend your time. Quitting is not making excuses, it's learning to be more productive, efficient and effective instead. Quitting is letting go of things (or people) that are sucking the life out of you so you can do more things that will bring you strength.
—Osayi Emokpae Lasisi

There came a time I finally gave up.

Listening to the doubts. Believing the lies. Holding on to the past.

Punishing myself. Making excuses. Hating myself. Giving up.

There came a time I finally surrendered.

My ego. My need to always be right. My selfishness. My weakness.

My fight against that I cannot control. My desire to please everyone. My anger. My crutches.

There came a time I finally quit.

Hiding my light. Fearing the leap. Blaming others. Sweating the small stuff.

Worrying what others might think. Denying my gifts. Quitting.

There comes a time.

April 2

*Destiny is not a matter of chance; it is a matter of choice. It is
not a thing to be waited for; it is a thing to be achieved.*
—William Jennings Bryan

There is a life I am after
I chase it endlessly
One filled with laughter
An ever-after happily

There is a dream I dream
It arrives every night
I am stronger than I seem
I never give up the fight

There is a place I am going
I am not there just yet
But I go forth knowing
I will arrive without regret

There is a day I am wanting
One day I will be free
The past no longer taunting
It is not my legacy

There is a choice I am making
To believe I have them already
They've been mine for the taking
For I get to choose my destiny.

April 3

It's not what we do once in a while that shapes our lives. It's what we do consistently.
—Anthony Robbins

How do you impart change upon anything?

Your behavior. Your relationships.
Your children. Your environment. Your career. Your future. Your life.

It simply comes down to this: Be consistent. Be insistent.

Consistent. Whatever changes you wish to see must begin with consistency. It must become a way of walking, talking, thinking, acting.

An active decision. Day in, day out. Habitual. Your routine. It must fit as if your second skin.

Until it is no longer a thought. It is simply the way you go about doing your business. As if breathing.

Insistent. Whatever changes you wish to see, you must be insistent upon. No excuses or exceptions.

Set the expectations. Define them. Make them clear. State them. Make them measurable. Then insist upon them.

The method for achieving them may be changed or altered along the way. This is flexibility. But there must always be integrity to the standard. This is insistency.

How do you impart change?

Be consistent. Be insistent.

April 4

If it is not on your calendar, it is not in your life.
—Unknown

Make the time

For longer walks
More gentle talks
Time with the young
Songs needing sung
Mending fences
Forgiving past tenses
A call to your mother
The hug for a brother
Thank you and please
A moment on your knees
That solitary run
Simply sitting in the sun
A leisurely drive
Whatever makes you feel alive
Lending a hand
Toes in the sand
An afternoon rest
Wearing your Sunday best
Fill a desire
Relax by the fire
Take that chance
A long, slow dance
Listening to the ocean
Quieting the commotion

Visiting the lonely
Being who you want to be
Smelling the roses
Rubbing noses
Petting puppies
Listening to the trees
Talks with your grandpa
Looking at life with awe
Making wishes
Butterfly kisses
Hugs that never end
Lemonade with a friend

Then take the time.

April 5

Be inspired, raising the bar of excellence in your life every day. Act better
than before; grow higher than usual; think faster than normal.
—Israelmore Ayivor

Life is simple.

Be kind.
Be humble.
Be grateful.
Raise your bar.

Give generously.
Give from the heart.
Give without condition.
Raise your bar.

Speak the gentle truth.
Speak with your heart.
Speak to lift another.
Raise your bar.

Do with peaceful intent.
Do to make a difference.
Do what is good and just.
Raise your bar.

Become a light.
Become a servant.
Become hope itself.
Raise your bar.

Act without malice.
Act as to always welcome others.
Act from a place of love.
Raise your bar.

Life is simple.
Be. Give. Speak. Do. Become. Act.
Raise your bar.

April 6

*If you wouldn't say those things to someone else you
love, why are you saying them to yourself?*
—Elaina Marie

Someone once glanced at my body and said, "You should be ashamed."

And I felt shame.

Someone once looked into my eyes and said, "You are not beautiful."

And I could not see my beauty.

Someone once spoke of my aspirations and said, "You will never amount to much."

And I believed.

Someone once laughed at my dreams and said, "You are foolish to believe."

And I no longer dreamed.

Someone once crept inside my thoughts and said, "You should be afraid."

And I was fearful.

Someone once talked to my heart and said, "You are not worthy of love."

And I was never good enough.

Someone once took measure of my life and said, "You are simply a failure."

And I lived up to this.

Someone was me. Once. These were my words. Once. But nevermore.

For I no longer give myself permission to speak this way.

Words I would not speak to another.

Words that do not serve my good.

Words so unloving.

Words that are not my truth.

April 7

I've been thinking about this a lot, and I think maybe it's true, even though I don't really like uncertainty. I'd much rather "know," but then again, not-knowing keeps all the possibilities open. It keeps all the worlds alive.
—Ruth Ozeki

I do not know how far I can go.

But I will never find out unless I move forward from this place.

I do not know how strong I need to be.

But I will never find out unless I address my weaknesses.

I do not know how brave I can become.

But I will never find out unless I turn to face my fears.

I do not know how I will handle being broken.

But I will never find out unless I push beyond my limits.

I do not know how I will answer all of life's questions.

But I will never find out unless I put myself to the test.

April 8

Don't let procrastination take over your life. Be brave and
take risks. Your life is happening right now.
—Roy Bennett

When the "have to" in your life becomes the "get to" in your life, you will understand the sheer power of gratitude.

When the "should" in your life becomes the "will" in your life, you will look back on these days without regret.

When the "need" in your life becomes the "want" in your life, you will embrace the freedom of choice.

When the "but" in your life becomes the "and" in your life, you will never again be overtaken by excuses.

When the "one day" in your life becomes the "today" in your life, you will be closer to the dream for your life.

April 9

*Faith to me is trusting in every evidence that something is—
that it is possible, that it is significant, that it is real.*
—Richelle E. Goodrich

I do not think about the tired beginning to settle in.

I simply trust I will find the finish.

I do not answer to the pain that is gathering.

I simply call on the strength that already exists.

I do not give credence to the notion I am bound by limits.

I simply have faith in my wings.

I do not ask how I will get up again.

I simply realize I have no other choice.

I do not consider whether I will succeed or not.

I simply believe in my ability not to fail.

April 10

Spread your arms in an embrace, throw your head back, and
prepare to receive and send coordinates of being. For, at last you
know—you are the navigator, the captain, and the ship.
—*Vera Nazarian*

Where are you willing to go?
Will you venture into the pain
Slowly dipping yourself in
Until you no longer feel numb?

Where are you willing to go?
Will you venture into the darkness
Allowing it to envelope you
Until you no longer are afraid?

Where are you willing to go?
Will you venture into the wilderness
Wandering so far from home
Until you no longer fear being lost?

Where are you willing to go?
Will you venture into the unknown
Beyond the safety of your comfort
Until you no longer cling to what used to be?

Where are you willing to go?
Will you venture unto the ledge
With no place left to turn
Until you no longer have a choice but to leap?

So tell me, my friend, where are you willing to go?

April II

*Many times what we perceive as an error or failure is actually
a gift. And eventually we find that lessons learned from that
discouraging experience prove to be of great worth.*
—Richelle E. Goodrich

For so long, I cowered before all that has made me who I am.

I cursed my fears. Angry, for they kept me paralyzed.

Never understanding they showed me where my courage lives.

I regretted my mistakes. Disappointed, for they kept me from success.

Never understanding they were my greatest teachers.

I avoided my pains. Numb, for they kept me vulnerable.

Never understanding they were measures of my strength.

I grew weary from the wanderings. Lost, for they led me down broken roads.

Never understanding they brought me home.

I dreaded the heartaches. Bitter, for they kept me broken.

Never understanding they led me toward my true love.

I have finally grown to understand. All I have ever faced has made me who I am.

Thus, today, I can simply be.

April 12

The empty spaces of your soul are the ones you search for, pray for and want so desperately to be filled. They are also the spaces that will never be filled, until you are ready to do something you have never done.
—Shannon L. Alder

Here's the plain, unvarnished, no-nonsense, tough-love truth.

You will not find happiness using misery as your compass.

And yet it is the instrument by which you steer your life.

You will not reach a place of strength using weakness as your crutch.

And yet it is what you lean upon to travel your road.

You will not overcome the wall of failure using excuses as your ladder.

And yet these are the rungs you desperately cling to.

You will not achieve new heights using fear as your copilot.

And yet it is flying your plane.

Something must be different.

And until you are open, willing, and ready to do different, nothing will change.

It's time to make a change.

April 13

If you feel lost, disappointed, hesitant, or weak, return to yourself, to who you are, here and now and when you get there, you will discover yourself, like a lotus flower in full bloom, even in a muddy pond, beautiful and strong.
—Masaru Emoto

Times I am a complete mess
It is just part of the process

Times I stumble during the dance
It is simply part of taking a chance

Times I get the lyrics wrong
It is still a part of my song

Times I am still so afraid
It is the part when courage is made

Times I know not where I'm going
It is part of being OK with not knowing

Times I question if I will ever fly
It is part of the voice saying, "Just try"

Times I do not trust me
It is all a part of learning to be

There will be times unfair and rough
It is then you learn that parts of you are strong enough.

April 14

I'm grateful for today. I'm stronger, braver, wiser.
—Tony Curl

I shall greet this day with a smile. For whatever it brings to me, I hold inside of me a joy that cannot be moved.

I shall greet this day with a wink. For whatever it brings to me, I hold inside of me a knowledge that I will be OK.

I shall greet this day with my head up. For whatever it brings to me, I hold inside of me a confidence that cannot be undone.

I shall greet this day with hope. For whatever it brings to me, I hold inside of me a faith that always sees me through.

I shall greet this day with patience. For whatever it brings to me, I hold inside of me a calm from which I will breathe.

I shall greet this day with strength. For whatever it brings me, I hold inside of me a truth that speaks of how strong I have always been.

I shall greet this day with arms wide open. For whatever it brings, I hold inside of me a gratitude for simply being given yet another day.

April 15

The only journey is the one within.
—Rainer Maria Rilke

I am turning inward
Seeking the silence
Quieting the doubt
That speaks to me

I am turning inward
Seeking the strength
Setting down the burden
That weakens me

I am turning inward
Seeking the courage
Casting aside fear
That limits me

I am turning inward
Seeking the light
Scattering the darkness
That surrounds me

I am turning inward
Seeking the truth
Disproving the lies
That define me

I am turning inward
For there, I shall find all I seek.

April 16

But what really matters is not what you believe but the
faith and conviction with which you believe...
—Knut Hamsun

Two words. Three letters. Big difference.

I have a dream, *but* I do not think I can achieve it.

I have a dream, *and* I will do what I need in order to achieve it.

I want to do this, *but* I have failed so many times before.

I want to do this, *and* if I fail again, I will try again.

I need to make some changes, *but* I am afraid of what that may bring.

I need to make some changes, *and* despite what that may bring, I know what I must do.

But or *and*. The choice is yours.

Choose well.

April 17

You have to really want and need it before you earn it.
—Toba Beta

Wandered through my darkness
Came away with a light

Spent time in my own dungeon
Walked away with a key

Dwelled in my pit of misery
Walked away with a rope

Broken by my own weakness
Walked away with a strength

Was down on my knees
Walked away with a prayer

And as I walked away
I came to realize all I have ever been through
Has given me all I shall ever need
For where I am now going.

April 18

Every shortcut has a price usually greater than the reward.
—Bryant McGill

There are no shortcuts
Each step on the path must be taken
This is perseverance

There are no U-turns
The path always leads forward
This is growth

There are no fast-forward buttons
You will arrive when you are ready
This is patience

There are no signs along the way
You must follow your heart
This is trust

There are no others who can walk your path
Only you know the way
This is your journey

April 19

As I looked out at the water, I realized there was nowhere to go, nowhere left to run. And I just had to stay here, facing this terrible truth. I felt, as more tears fell, just how tired I was, a tiredness that had nothing to do with the hour. I was tired of running away from this, tired of not telling people, tired of not talking about it, tired of pretending things were okay when they had never, ever been less than okay.
—Morgan Matson

I am tired.

Tired of standing on the ledge
Today, I take a leap of faith

I am tired.

Tired of clinging to that which no longer serves my good
Today, I simply let go

I am tired.

Tired of wondering what may be
Today, I move forward unafraid of the not knowing

I am tired.

Tired of the worries, doubts, and fears that fill my spaces
Today, I clean house

I am tired.

Tired of being tired
Today, I awake to live the life I am worthy of

April 20

It is the time you have wasted for your rose that makes your rose so important.
—Antoine de Saint-Exupéry

Time. I cannot slow it down. Yet should I allow, there shall be moments that brilliantly stand still.

Time. I cannot gather it up to be saved as a treasure. Yet should I allow, there shall be moments that collect as precious gifts.

Time. I cannot borrow more than I am afforded. Yet should I allow, there shall be moments that steal the breath given me.

Time. I cannot define its boundaries. Yet should I allow, there shall be moments that define me.

Time. For although it is not mine to own, it is all I have. And, thus, I have made my choice as to how I shall spend it.

I shall not let it be wasted on the petty, useless, or negative.

I shall breathe in each moment until I am filled with gratitude.

I shall not wish it away or regret where it leads me.

I shall not pray for more but pray I lived in all the moments I have.

I shall honor its passing with grace.

April 21

There are tests, but there are also small mercies. Life tossed us up into the air,
scattered us, and we all somehow found our way back. And we will do it again.
And again. And again.
—Alexandra Bracken

What do you do when your body feels tired, old, and broken, betraying your desire?

You find a way to listen to your heart.

What do you do when the questions outnumber the answers?

You find a way to simply believe.

What do you do when the hurt arrives, settling into your being?

You find a way to stay strong.

What do you do when the unknown stretches vast and dark before you?

You find a way to move to the light.

What do you do when the time comes to face the challenge rising before you?

You find a way to be bigger than the moment.

What do you do when standing at the precipice and all your fears and doubts scream your name?

You find a way to jump.

You find a way. It's what you do.

April 22

Do you wake up as I do, having forgotten what it is that hurts or where, until you move? There is a second of consciousness that is clean again. A second that is you, without memory or experience, the animal warm and waking into a brand new world. There is the sun dissolving the dark, and light as clear as music, filling the room where you sleep and the other rooms behind your eyes.
—Jeanette Winterson

Today, when I woke up, I still felt so very weary.

Today, when I woke up, I realized I am not where I want to be.

Today, when I woke up, I struggled with the ache my heart has come to know.

Today, when I woke up, I doubted my strength to see me through.

Today, when I woke up, I questioned where this path shall lead me.

Today, when I woke up, I sat with the same fears I've been haunted by for so long.

Today, I woke up. The rest is just details.

April 23

The individual has always had to struggle to keep from being overwhelmed
by the tribe. If you try it, you will be lonely often, and sometimes frightened.
But no price is too high to pay for the privilege of owning yourself.
—*Friedrich Nietzsche*

I have taken a knee out of weakness.

This, the price paid for seeking strength.

I have felt paralyzing fear.

This, the price paid for living at the edge of comfort.

I have often experienced failure.

This, the price paid for living in pursuit of my dreams.

I have been wounded.

This, the price paid for living as a warrior.

I have known brokenness.

This, the price paid for living with a heart open and exposed.

I have become me. A strong yet gentle soul. A wanderer. A dreamer. A warrior.

This, the reward for paying the price.

April 24

Man often becomes what he believes himself to be. If I keep on saying to myself that I cannot do a certain thing, it is possible that I may end by really becoming incapable of doing it. On the contrary, if I have the belief that I can do it, I shall surely acquire the capacity to do it even if I may not have it at the beginning.
—Mahatma Gandhi

I am capable of all I believe. Deep within the recesses of my thoughts.

May I forever be mindful to stay positive in thought.

I am capable of all I envision. Deep within the dreams I hold most dear.

May I forever dare to dream big.

I am capable of all I desire. Deep within the chambers of this warrior's heart.

May I forever move toward that which makes my heart beat faster.

I am capable of all I speak. Deep within the words I whisper to myself.

May I forever be gentle with all words spoken of me.

I am capable. And when I embrace this simple truth, nothing is impossible.

April 25

At that darkest moment, while drowning in the Abyss of Emotional Bankruptcy, reflect on this universal truth: the difference between success and failure is one more time.
—Ken Poirot

When I thought I could not go on
I took but one more step

When I thought I could not rise again
I stood but one more time

When I thought I could not succeed
I gave but one more try

When I thought I could not reach a dream
I closed my eyes one more time

When I thought I could not be healed
I felt my heart give one more beat

The power of one more. It is within you.

April 26

Seeking excellence means choosing to forge your own sword to cut through the limitations of your life...
—James A. Murphy

Today does not define me.

How I choose determines who I am.

The challenges I may face today will not define me.

How I choose to handle myself during times of struggle determines who I am.

The failures I may face today will not define me.

How I choose to continue on after knowing defeat determines who I am.

The questions I may face today will not define me.

How I choose to respond to the unknowns determines who I am.

The fear I may face today will not define me.

How I choose to steady myself when I am afraid determines who I am.

I always get to choose.

April 27

Listen to the mustn'ts, child. Listen to the don'ts. Listen to the shouldn'ts,
the impossibles, the won'ts. Listen to the never haves, then listen
close to me...Anything can happen, child. Anything can be.
—Shel Silverstein

If you ask when my impossible became possible, I would tell you this.

It happened when

...my excuses no longer outweighed my priorities

...my fears no longer spoke my truth

...my tears no longer exceeded my sweat

...my failures no longer defined my path

...my won't no longer was a match for my will

...my comfort zone no longer held my dreams

...my life no longer could wait for whenever.

April 28

How many of us stop short of success on purpose? How many of us sabotage
our own happiness because failure, while miserable, is a fear we're familiar with?
Success, however, dreams come true, are a whole new kind of terrifying, an entire
new species of responsibilities and disillusions, requiring a new way to think, act
and become. Why do we really quit? Because it's hopeless? Or because it's possible?
—Jennifer DeLucy

There are two sides to the coin known as fear: failing or succeeding.

Both sides are real. Both sides exist for us all. Both sides are equally limiting.

But what is important to know is the sides are not polar opposites. In fact, they are both born of a simple misunderstanding. And they are linked to a mind-set we carry about ourselves.

Fear of failing. The simple misunderstanding that failure is not a state of permanence. The misconception that we are not permitted mistakes, do-overs, setbacks. Believing in the mind-set that success is for others.

Fear of succeeding. The simple misunderstanding that success is not meant for us. The misconception that we are somehow not deserving, worthy, or capable. Believing in the mind-set that we are destined to fail.

Thus, if we are to overcome either side of fear, we must alter our thinking and long-held beliefs about ourselves.

We are allowed to make mistakes. We have a right to keep trying until we figure this thing out.

We are worthy of success. We have a right to the light, love, and life that is meant for us.

April 29

I'm not lost, just undiscovered.
—James Morrison

Thought I was lost. For a life turned upside down.

Was simply discovering the strength to stand up once again.

Thought I was lost. For the many failures I have known.

Was simply discovering the keys to my success.

Thought I was lost. For times driven to my knees.

Was simply discovering answers to my prayers.

Thought I was lost. For the roads I have aimlessly wandered.

Was simply discovering the path that leads me home.

Thought I was lost. For all the missing pieces.

Was simply discovering that which makes me complete.

I'm not lost. Just undiscovered.

April 30

If you look for perfection, you'll never be content.
—Leo Tolstoy

I got lost along the path, chasing after you
Were you just a mirage or something true?
Always in sight, yet never did I embrace
Never where I stood, you were in another place
I sought you out, called out your very name
You were more valuable than riches or fame
Called to you in a whispered tone, or was it a scream?
Became lost in a nightmare while chasing a dream.

Lost my sense of direction searching for you
Forgot so much of what I already knew
Lost my very self, my soul and heart
Trying to hold you, my world was falling apart
It was perfection that which I sought
Hard and painful were the lessons taught
As I chased after you, so much was lost
Never will I know the ultimate cost.

Yet there is value in the lesson learned
A sense of contentment I have earned
Progress is where I find happiness
Seeking perfection produced only stress
Thought I needed to be a perfect version of me
Hoped my flaws and scars no others could see
Denied and hated my failures for so very long
Not knowing they helped me grow strong.

Finally found peace when I let go of the chase
Found myself at home, standing in this place
Embracing all that I am and all I will never be
I found my breath, found my voice, found the true me
I am not perfect, nor do I need to be
I see my scars, I see my faults, I see me.
I will continue to strive to become and to grow
Yet finally free, the burden of perfect no longer in tow.

I am imperfectly and simply me
It is who I am ultimately supposed to be
I love the best of me, I love the rest of me
Ironic, I can finally love myself...perfectly.

May 1

*When we do not succeed to be ourselves, we finally realize that it was
completely useless to exist...*
—Hugo Pratt

When the fear arrives, calling your name

There can be but one response. Simply be you.

When the doubt arrives, questioning your faith

There can be but one response. Simply be you.

When the weakness arrives, shouting you can't do this

There can be but one response. Simply be you.

When the storm arrives, howling before you

There can be but one response. Simply be you.

When the pain arrives, demanding you surrender

There can be but one response. Simply be you.

When the truth arrives, it will already know how you made it through.

You were simply you. Brave. Confident. Strong. Calm. Unbreakable.

May 2

That word is "willing." It's an attitude and spirit of cooperation that should permeate our conversations. It's like a palm tree by the ocean that endures the greatest winds because it knows how to gracefully bend.
—Stephen Kendrick

My greatest struggle.

Is it an inability or unwillingness that does not allow me

To trust, to change, to grow?

To forgive, to make amends, to let go?

To accept, to believe, to know peace?

To heal, to surrender, to just be OK?

To rejoice in me, to honor my gifts, to fully love myself?

But when I am honest and open and real, I know what keeps me from this to-do list.

It has never been my inability.
It comes from a place of unwillingness.

Rooted in worn excuses, a past no longer serving me and the drone of a voice that continues to not speak my truth.

If I am to move from this place, the most powerful words I can speak to myself today: "I am willing. I am able."

And the struggle is not so great.

May 3

The primary cause of unhappiness is never the situation, but your thoughts about it. Be aware of the thoughts you are thinking.
—Eckhart Tolle

I thought I was lost
Never to find my way
It was not worth the cost
To search again today

I thought I was broken
Never to again heal
Soothing words not spoken
The pain was too real

I thought I could not go on
Never to know success
The fight simply gone
Willing to settle for less

My thoughts were wrong
I know the way to go
Understood all along
Simply forgot what I know

My thoughts were untrue
I hold the healing power
From this point of view
I refuse to cower

My thoughts were a lie
I can and will continue on
Spread my wings and fly
To face another dawn

This one is for you
You are not lost
You are not broken
You can go on.

May 4

Life has a way of taking you past your wants and hopes.
Instead, it drops you in front of what you need.
—Shannon L. Alder

Life offers what I need. This. Another life chat.

Me: I want yesterday back. Before the brokenness found me.
Life: I cannot offer that.

Me: I want yesterday back. Before the emptiness settled upon me.
Life: I cannot offer that.

Me: I want yesterday back. Before the darkness enveloped me.
Life: I cannot offer that.

Me: I want yesterday back. Before the happiness dissipated before me.
Life: I cannot offer that.

Me: I want yesterday back. Before the truth was ripped from me.
Life: I cannot offer that.

Me: I want yesterday back. Before the life I knew unraveled before me.
Life: I cannot offer that.

Me: What, then, can you offer me?
Life: At times not what you want but always what you need.

Me: When shall I find what I need?
Life: When you stop looking behind you, what you need waits in the distance.

Me: What is waiting there for me?
Life: Healing. Peace. Light. Joy. Forgiveness. Love.

Me: How ever shall I arrive there?
Life: Simply invite it home. It will come to you.

May 5

Try—now's gift.
—H. L. Balcomb

Life will make you fight for it
Fight the voices in your head
Whispering for you to quit
Fight the resignation, fight the dread

Life won't always play fair
But it expects a good fight
For excuses it doesn't care
It expects you to get it right

Life doesn't care if you're tired
It wants to know if you'll try
You must fight for what's desired
Or it will pass you by

Life will knock you to your knees
Then expect you to stand
When quitting would be a breeze
"Try again," it will demand.

May 6

Did I offer peace today? Did I bring a smile to someone's face? Did I say
words of healing? Did I let go of my anger and resentment? Did I forgive? Did
I love? These are the real questions. I must trust that the little bit of love that
I sow now will bear many fruits, here in this world and the life to come.
—Henri Nouwen

Did you watch the sunrise
Allow beauty to come your way?
Did you gaze in your child's eyes
And see joy as if Christmas Day?

Did you hear the song of the birds
Accepting their invitation to dance?
Did you reach for kinder words?
In every breath a new chance

Did you feel the morning still
How it quietly moved the night?
Did you find it in your will
To quietly continue to fight?

Did you taste the new start
The nectar each new day brings?
Did you place hand upon heart?
It contains your set of wings

Did you accept the gift of today
Much grander than it seems?
Did you agree to be on your way
To once again chase your dreams?

Did you?

May 7

*Even in times of trauma, we try to maintain a sense of normality until
we no longer can. That, my friends, is called surviving. Not healing. We
never become whole again...we are survivors. If you are here today...
you are a survivor. But those of us who have made it through hell
and are still standing? We bear a different name: warriors.*
—Lori Goodwin

Have traveled my way alone
Until hope seemed gone
Times weary to the bone
Yet still I kept moving on

In the darkness became lost
Fearful I would never get home
But standing still a greater cost
So I continued to roam

Been on this journey
This road so very long
What I failed to see
With each step I grew strong

Been wrong more than right
Failures, I have known many
I will not give up the fight
For I must be true to me

Was bruised and bloodied
Pain forced to endure
Broken, I did not concede
That's when I became a warrior.

May 8

It's like there are a million screams caught inside of my chest but I have to keep them all in because what's the point of screaming, if you'll never be heard and no one will ever hear me?
—Tahereh Mafi

Screamed out loud
Alone silently wept
Can anyone hear
A heart breaking?

Again going under
Waves crashing down
Can anyone save
A soul drowning?

Lost in the crowd
Yet no one near
Can anyone reach
A wayward spirit?

Trapped by thoughts
Tormenting
Can anyone free
A shackled mind?

Came the answer
When the noise faded
As the waves broke
In the solitude

Hope hears all
Faith saves all
Love reaches all
Peace frees all

May 9

"I wear the chain I forged in life," replied the Ghost. "I made it link by link, and yard by yard; I girded it on of my own free will, and of my own free will I wore it."
—Charles Dickens

Break the chain
Against doubt rage
Refuse to remain
In your imaginary cage

When limits you own
Difficult to fully become
Beyond your comfort zone
There is much freedom

You are not bound
The cage is open wide
Get up off the ground
Then simply step outside

Of that which fear paints
You have always been free
The illusion of restraints
For in your hands, the key

What are you waiting for?
Go with arm wide open
For life is an open door
Waiting for you to begin

May 10

Life is not a search for answers but the answer itself.
—Marty Rubin

The answer is simple:
Show up
Rise up
Never give up

The answer is simple:
Give your best
Give a little more
Give all you have

The answer is simple:
Work hard
Play hard
Don't be so hard on yourself

The answer is simple:
Be strong
Be brave
Be yourself

The answer is simple:
Without excuse
Without regret
Without harm

The answer is simple:
Leave no doubt
Leave the tank empty
Leave nothing to chance

The answer is simple:
Honestly
Gratefully
Hopefully

The question: how do I live?

May 11

It is hard to fail, but it is worse never to have tried to succeed.
—Theodore Roosevelt

I have lost. Many times.

Lost my way. Lost loves. Lost hope. Lost my sense of purpose.

But not once did I ever stop searching.

And, thus, so much have I discovered.

I have fallen. Many times.

Into the abyss. Over things grand and small. In holes dug by my own hands.

But not once did I refuse to rise to my feet.

And, thus, how high I have climbed.

I have failed. Many times.

Failed in school. Failed at jobs. Failed in relationships. Failed to reach goals and dreams.

But not once did I ever give up.

And, thus, I came to realize I was merely learning how to succeed.

May 12

There is a lie in between a promise and many excuses.
—Toba Beta

Excuses were everywhere
So very easy to find
Found them waiting there,
Ready to change my mind

Kept on the nightstand
In the morning they awoke
Changed what I planned
For so loudly they spoke

In the mirror they appeared
Your best days are passed
Could it be true, I feared,
Excuses are all that last?

Written in the calendar
Of time they were a thief
Goals became a blur
For excuses altered belief

One day I listened no longer
For I began to finally see
The truth is much stronger
My excuses had failed me

In the mirror someone new
Excuses do not define me
For they are not true
Knowing this, I am set free

My excuses I did erase
Time to write a new song
They cannot occupy space
Where my dreams belong

May 13

Great men are not born great; they grow great...
—Mario Puzo

Do not simply anticipate
Go out and make your great
Today a new opportunity
To realize how great you can be

Imagine what you can achieve
If in your greatness you believe
There is no wall you cannot scale
Comes belief, you cannot fail.

Dare to soar
Dare to roar
Head up, shoulders proud
Live this day out loud.

Announce you did arrive
Do more than just survive.
This day is another chance
To create your own dance.

Today may you celebrate
Today make your great
Greatness not just for some
Take your place at the podium.

So show up and be strong
Greatness is coming along
Do not continue to wait
Go ahead and make your great

May 14

If you fell down yesterday, stand up today.
—H. G. Wells

When all else fails
And life empties your sails
You must be your own force
Allow yourself a new course

When the shore seems too far
And you wonder where you are
You must remain afloat
Trust is your lifeboat

When obstacles appear
And failure seems near
You must find your strong
Adjust and move along

When a heart is broken
And comes a pain unspoken
You must embrace the feeling
Very soon comes the healing

When you can't take anymore
Hopelessness is at the door
You must dig so very deep
It is hope you must keep

When comes a brand-new day
Know that there's always a way
Keep a belief in your heart
Today is when you finally start

May 15

If you've got nothing to dance about, find a reason to sing.
—Melody Carstairs

In the coldness of the morning, I rolled over and reached out for you. Like an old blanket, an old friend, I could always count on you to wrap me up and provide me comfort. Yet today I could not feel you.

You were my doubts, the blanket I wrapped around me to keep me safe. Safe from trying, safe from failing, safe from being hurt. I no longer need you. For I am warmed by a new sense of believing. Belief in me.

In the silence of the morning, I called out for you. Like a lullaby or familiar tune, I expected to hear your soothing voice. Yet today I could not hear you.

You were the voice that said, "I am not good enough," and I knew this refrain well. A chorus I used to sing myself to sleep. I no longer hear you. For I listen to a new voice of truth. "I am more than enough." It now sings to me.

In the darkness of the morning, I stumbled around searching for you. Like a light to guide my path, I needed you to show me the way. Yet today I could not see you.

You were my fears, and you lit the narrow path I walked. Fear that kept me from walking a new path. Fear that kept me surrounded by darkness. I no longer see you. For a new light shines brightly. A light of hope and trust.

In the waking of the morning, I simply waited for you. But you never came. And I realized I am finally alone. Yet today I am going to be OK without you.

Today I wish for you a day without doubt, without negative self-talk, without fear. Donate that blanket of doubt. Turn down the volume of that voice. Walk in a new light.

There is so much in you to believe in. Your strength and courage. Your gifts and love. Your heart and soul. You.

There is another voice to listen to. One that speaks gently of your beauty and light. One that praises your goodness and worth. One that sings of your treasures. You.

There is a new light to see. A light of hope and happiness. A light of renewal and reinvention. A light of becoming. You.

Believe. Sing. Shine.

May 16

Today I choose life. Every morning when I wake up I can choose joy, happiness, negativity, pain...To feel the freedom that comes from being able to continue to make mistakes and choices—today I choose to feel life, not to deny my humanity but embrace it.
—Kevyn Aucoin

In the silence of the new day, what do you hear:
"I can't" or "I can"?
"I am not enough" or "I am immeasurable"?
"I have failed" or "I will succeed"?

In the breaking of the morning's light, what do you see:
The shadows of regret or the dawn of acceptance?
Sorrow's darkness or joy's brilliance?
The blackness of fear or the amazing colors of hope?

In the calm of the day's beginning, what do you feel:
A paralysis of doubt or the movement that comes with belief?
The stress of want or the stillness of contentment?
Half empty or fully alive?

In the waking to this day, what do you taste:
Bitterness of mistakes or the sweetness of forgiveness?
Staleness of yesterday or the bold flavor of today?
Nothing from an empty cup or everything, for your cup overflows?

My wish for you today:

May your words to yourself be always gentle and loving.

May your heart see your true beauty and worth.

May you breathe in calmness and strength and breathe out peace and courage.

May you taste the richness of all this day has in store for you.

May your senses completely tingle.

May 17

I, not events, have the power to make me happy or unhappy today. I can choose
which it shall be. I have just one day, today, and I'm going to be happy in it.
—*Groucho Marx*

Here are some simple observations to help you go get today:

1. When you're standing tall, reach higher.

2. Falling down happens. Staying down is a choice.

3. Everyone gets weary. Everyone breaks. It is not a sign of weakness but of humanness.

4. When you fall down, get back up. Every time.

5. When the weight gets too heavy, it's OK to put it down.

6. When obstacles appear in your way, jump with both feet.

7. Some obstacles you'll have to overcome more than once. That's OK. Been there. Done that. You can do it again.

8. If you feel yourself coming a little undone, take a moment, tuck yourself in, and then start again.

9. A challenge, by its very nature, is meant to be difficult. Life is a challenge.

10. You are never alone. Others understand what you are going through. Call upon them.

May 18

When I hear somebody sigh, "Life is hard," I am always tempted to ask,
"Compared to what?"
—Sydney J. Harris

It sometimes is a struggle.
I have known hardships.

It can feel bigger than my ability.
I have failed often.

It can wear me down.
I have felt the weariness.

It scares me at times.
I have walked in fear.

It demands so much of me.
I have found the wall.

It pushes me to the breaking.
I have been down on my knees.

It isn't always pretty.
I have the scars.

This. It is my life.
Despite all of the above.

I will take it.

May 19

A lifetime isn't forever, so take the first chance, don't wait for the second one! Because sometimes, there aren't second chances! And if it turns out to be a mistake? So what! This is life! A whole bunch of mistakes! But if you never get a second chance at something you didn't take a first chance at? That's true failure.
—C. JoyBell C.

If given the chance to leap
I shall jump without fear

If given the chance to fail
I shall not let it define me

If given the chance to forgive
I shall forgive without expectation

If given the chance to love again
I shall love unconditionally

If given the chance to dance
I shall dance to the song in my heart

If given the chance to dream
I shall dream the impossible

If given the chance to live but once
I shall honor the life I have been given

Each and every day
You are given the chance

Leap without fear
Fail without being defined
Forgive without expectation
Love unconditionally
Dance to your heart's song
Dream the impossible

Take the chance.

May 20

*Bad things do happen; how I respond to them defines my character
and the quality of my life. I can choose to sit in perpetual sadness,
immobilized by the gravity of my loss, or I can choose to rise from
the pain and treasure the most precious gift I have—life itself.*
—Walter Anderson

I cannot silence the voices of doubt.

I can only make sure they are not spoken from me.

I cannot forget the road that led me here.

I can only forgive myself for the missteps I took.

I cannot unwind the tangles of yesterday.

I can only prepare myself to not come unwound today.

I cannot let go by clinging so tightly.

I can only know peace by unclenching my fist.

I cannot undo what has been done.

I can only do what now must be done.

It is rarely about what I cannot do that determines my fate

But, rather, what I can do.

May 21

I can and I will.
—Nadiya Hussain

I can get back up again
I will find the strength

I can find the strength
I will push beyond my limits

I can push beyond my limits
I will not accept my excuses

I cannot accept my excuses
I will believe in my truth

I can believe in my truth
I will see my own worth

I can see my own worth
I will treat myself as worthy

I can treat myself as worthy
I will do what is best for me

I can do what is best for me
I will make today the day.

May 22

The higher we soar, the smaller we appear to those who cannot fly.
—Friedrich Nietzsche

Against the cage
You must rage
The spirit does die
When unable to fly
Born to soar
Bound no more
Given wings
The heart sings
Tethered to the ground
It makes no sound
Fear not the height
Simply take flight
You've been gifted
Your soul lifted
They know not why
You were born to fly
Do not give mind
What they cannot find
Mind not their lack of sight
Simply take flight
No longer small
Risen above it all
Wait nevermore
Time to soar.

May 23

The world as we have created it is a process of our thinking. It
cannot be changed without changing our thinking.
—Albert Einstein

No longer wanted to feel sad
Life really is not so bad
Just like that, changed my way
Decided to be happy again today

No longer wanted to feel the pain
For too long the hurt did drain
Just like that, changed what I feel
Decided I am allowed to heal

No longer wanted to shed a tear
The longing brought irrational fear
Just like that, changed my cry
Decided to give love another try

No longer wanted to feel dread
Feeling half alive, half dead
Just like that, changed my course
Decided to live life full force

Came to finally understand
Things may never go as planned
Yet this life is always mine
Each day I ultimately design

I woke up again today
Willing to change my way
Given another turn at bat
Changed, just like that.

May 24

Whatever you do be gentle with yourself. You don't just live in this world or your home or your skin. You also live in someone's eyes.
—Sanober Khan

Been searching for that one true soul
To see the diamonds through my coal
A special one to set me free
Someone to finally see me for me

Searching, I have traveled many a road
Hoping for someone to ease my load
A special one to wipe the tears
Someone to see past my fears

Seeking that one to illuminate my stars
Someone to look beyond my scars
For hidden deep is my beauty
Could anyone find it buried in me?

As another day came to an end
My prayers again I did send
Send to me one who could see my possibility
The one to see the gifts in me

And as a new dawn did break
Someone was waiting as I did awake
For when I looked in the mirror, who should I see?
That someone was staring back at me

For our single intent each day
See ourselves in a special way
To begin to see our own beauty
Until then, few will be able to see

So stand before the glass
Not another day should pass
It is time you finally knew
That someone is looking back at you.

May 25

Close some doors today. Not because of pride, incapacity or arrogance,
but simply because they lead you nowhere.
—Paulo Coelho

Close the door of regret
Unable to hold what you did not get
Let go of that handle
Regret is a flame of an unlit candle

Close the door to the past
Let go of that never meant to last
The past is merely a ghost
The spirit of today matters most

Close the door to the pain
Dry tears that once did stain
The hurt you felt once so real
Time to allow yourself to heal

Close the door to all untrue
The lies will never define you
Believe in that which you know
What is false you must let go

Close the door to your fear
Just illusions that never appear
Fear is a great falsehood
Let go, they serve no good

Beyond the doors you close
What awaits no one knows
What you are hoping to find
Is not found looking behind

Take the time to close it tight
Resist opening it with all your might
Find the locking key
The key that sets you free

And as you turn the key
To all not meant to be
A new door will unlock
Step to it, give it a knock.

May 26

*You are your own refuge. There is no other. You cannot
save another. You can only save yourself.*
—Guillaume Musso

On this day let me pen
I did not play it safe again
On this day let me risk it all
Knowing I am not afraid to fall

Throw my arms wide open today
Not fearing what others may say
Take the leap into the abyss
No more chances will I miss

Dare once more to touch the sky
Trust that I will learn to fly
Let my very spirit take flight
Do not grip my fears so tight

Experience this amazing life
Complete with all its strife
Let me find my brave
For another day will not save

I am beginning my life today
Despite the risks in the way
I am braver than I know
Today, courage will I show

Does not mean I am unafraid
Inside know of what I am made
Heart, tenacity, fight, and grit
Spunk, fire, not a hint of quit

At the end of the day
Let me quietly say
I lived my brave
Myself I save.

May 27

Stop trying to fix yourself; you're not broken! You are perfectly imperfect
and powerful beyond measure.
—Steve Maraboli

Four words must be spoken
"I am not broken"
You're not made of porcelain
Your scars tell where you've been

They do not need to be hidden
Mistakes should not be forbidden
Time to rethink and reflect
You don't have to be perfect

Three words should be taught
Simply repeat, "I am not"
Fill in the blank as you need
Let "I am not" be your creed

I am not defined by my past
This pain will not last
I am not afraid of today
I can let go of yesterday

Two simple words to say
To help you get out of your way
When life becomes a difficult exam
Simply answer, "I am"

I am
I am not

I am who I am supposed to be
I do not need anyone to fix me
I am OK with who I am
Thinking otherwise is a scam

One word holds all the power
Above all others let it tower
Yet so reluctant to give it a try
You find peace when you say, "I"

I will ask for what I need
My own soul I will feed
I love me and all I may be
This alone sets me free.

May 28

I walk slowly, but I never walk backward.
—Abraham Lincoln

Walking toward something I do not know
But forward I must continue to go
There is nothing waiting ahead of me
Which in the rearview mirror I still see

Walking toward a new horizon
Yesterday is said and done
Walking away from the past
Even if I am not walking fast

And as I slowly walk away
I grow stronger each and every day
If I simply keep moving along
I will one day learn to run strong

On this lonely walkabout
Comes the fear, comes the doubt
With your back to the sun, shadows appear
No need to run away from your fear

Just walk forward, and before the day is done
You will be walking toward the sun
Walk to the light, and you will find
Shadows and fears get left behind

Walk slowly if you must
And with every step trust
You are on the right track
You are not walking back.

May 29

That is what learning is. You suddenly understand something you've
understood all your life, but in a new way.
—Doris Lessing

On failing: I've learned failing simply means I get to try again.

On fear: I've learned most of what I fear never actually happens.

On pain: I've learned it hurts more when I keep thinking about it.

On happiness: I've learned it is simply an invitation waiting to be accepted.

On strength: I've learned there is always enough to do what must be done.

On success: I've learned success is not an outcome but a process.

On growth: I've learned it is inevitable but easier when I accept the lessons put before me.

On today: I've learned it has no attachment to yesterday. It accepts me where I am.

On learning: I've learned I still have so much to learn.

May 30

When you choose hope, anything is possible.
—Christopher Reeve

Hope does not stop the darkness
It allows us to find the light

Hope does not ease the pain
It allows us strength to endure

Hope does not relieve us of hardships
It allows us courage to face them

Hope does not change the past
It allows us to make tomorrow better

Hope does not dry the tears
It allows us a reason to smile

Hope does not quiet the fears
It allows us to hear our heartbeat

Hope does not break down walls
It allows us to see beyond them

When you choose hope
Everything is possible.

May 31

Believe that you are someone worth saving.
—Slade Combs

Ever feel like you cannot win?
All the waves come crashing in
Constantly being pulled under
Dreams broken asunder

Waves rolling one after another
Too many, they begin to smother
Struggle to the surface to take in air
Fearing you will not make it there

The struggle begins to take a toll
Fear settles into your very soul
You cannot keep above the wave
Drowning, yourself you cannot save

When all else fails, simply float
You are your own lifeboat
Equipped with a built-in life vest
It beats strong inside your chest

Above the waves your head you must keep
Simply stand up, the water is but waist deep
And should it rise higher, do not flail of life and limb
You have always known how to swim

So jump in with both feet
Splash around, feel your heartbeat
Dare to swim away from shore
You can handle this and so much more

You have not been set adrift
You have received a gift
For every wave that comes along
Simply helps you grow strong.

June 1

Yesterday's home runs don't win today's games.
—Babe Ruth

The cruel irony of today
It cares not what came before
If today had its way
It would expect even more

For yesterday did come and go
And no matter what was done
Today simply wants to know:
What happens under this sun?

Today is another mountain peak
A climb that may seem so very long
Yesterday you might have been weak
Today expects you to be strong

Yesterday you might have been great
Today does not really care
It will not hesitate
To pose another test so unfair

What today does not know:
You are ready for the test
For you are ready to go
And give today your very best

So hit it high and hit it deep
Today will soon enough see
All the promises you will keep
As you earn another victory.

June 2

I attribute my success to this—I never gave or took any excuse.
—Florence Nightingale

When the hard times come
Your excuses will not excuse you from them

When the steps become difficult
Your "I cannot" will not suddenly become your "I can"

When the pain slowly creeps in
Your "I give up" will not give you the strength to overcome it

What will get you through the hard times
Are all the times you said, "I will"

What will get you through the difficult steps
Are the countless steps that led you there

What will get you through the pain
Are all the days you decided to get back up again

Do the work

Say you will

Take the steps

Get back up.

June 3

Always go with the choice that scares you the most, because that's the
one that is going to require the most from you.
—Caroline Myss

Arms wide open, a choice I'm making
Embracing all that comes my way
Each morning as I am waking
Accepting of what awaits this day

With arms spread so wide
I am finally free to let go
Of all I have so long denied
So I may begin to grow

Eyes wide open, a choice I'm making
Seeing the dawn of a new day
Aware of all the steps I am taking
I have finally found my way

With eyes wide open, I can now see
A light where darkness once appeared
A vision of who I can truly be
No longer afraid of what I feared

Heart wide open, a choice I'm making
To once again feel its gentle beat
Willing to risk again the breaking
To once again feel complete

With a heart worn on my sleeve
Comes the risk of deep pains
But I simply choose to believe
In the end, love is what remains.

June 4

No matter the situation, remind yourself, "I have a choice."
—Deepak Chopra

Dear Self,

This day, I am making the choice to believe in the possibility, believe in the process, believe in me.

This day, I am making the choice to walk a new path, walk away from the negative, walk with my head held high.

This day, I am making the choice to chase my dreams, stop chasing what is not good for me, chase away the doubt.

This day, I am making the choice to make amends, make new mistakes, make today count.

This day, I am making the choice to be positive, be happy, be at peace.

This day, I am making the choice to live out loud, live in a way that honors me, live life full force.

This day, I am making the choice to love where I am, love all of me, love my life.

Love, Me

June 5

Sometimes the most important thing in a whole day is the rest we
take between two deep breaths.
—*Etty Hillesum*

Breathe slowly and deeply
A moment to slow your pace
Allow yourself to simply be
Let calmness fill the space

When tension begins to rise
And the day starts to spin
Take time to close your eyes
And take a deep breath in

For in each breath made
A chance to start anew
To allow trouble to fade
To face what you must do

And as you exhale out
Trust what you know
Let go of the doubt
Fear can no longer grow

For you gave it no air
You gave it no space
Peace found everywhere
As you slow your pace

Breathe in ever slow
Take that gentle rest
Breathe out and go
Do your very best.

June 6

If we're growing, we're always going to be out of our comfort zone.
—John C. Maxwell

This is my comfort zone
The place I have made
The place that I own
Because I am afraid

Here, I stand my ground
Eyes closed so I cannot see
Fearful what may be found
Yet also blind to what may be

I thought it served me well
This place of safety
Instead it was a private hell
Kept me from being free

It has become my prison
Built by fear and doubt
I did not know how to begin
To let myself out

Behind this prison wall
I no longer want to stay
Should I stumble or fall
I must be on my way

I know where I must begin
The single key to freedom
Find comfort in my own skin
Allow myself to simply become

And with this knowing
I have already grown
Free to be going
Beyond my comfort zone.

June 7

We grow neither better nor worse as we get old, but more like ourselves.
—May Lamberton Becker

I'm growing to be more like me
A new picture for the shelf
For these eyes to finally see
One that reflects my true self

Been thinking I need to change
On myself been so tough
My thoughts I must rearrange
I've always been good enough

Tried to better myself for so long
Feared simply being who I am
All those messages were so wrong
Finally decided to delete that spam

The critic in me was the worst
Rarely, if ever, satisfied
From that voice no longer cursed
Learned to quiet the noise inside

I'm growing to be more like me
In the mirror a new reflection
And I love who I now see
Me and all my imperfection.

June 8

I dare you, while there is still time, to have a magnificent obsession.
—William Danforth

Have a magnificent obsession
Live a life so amazing
Keep dreams in possession
Set your soul a-blazing

Do all that which you love
Passionately do what you do
Become all you're thinking of
Fall in love again with you

Not grow weary of the chase
Believe in the path you are on
Create beauty in this place
Not look back once you've gone

Always make the time
Take the time for some fun
Always enjoy the climb
Never quit until it is done

A sense of wonder regain
Rejoice in things so small
Have gratitude remain
Extend your thanks to all

Be one who leads the way
For others, light the course
Shine so bright this day
Live life full force.

June 9

Children are happy because they don't have a file in their minds called
"All the things that could go wrong."
—*Marianne Williamson*

Every day you make your list
It has grown so very long
On keeping this file you insist
All the things that can go wrong

Not a file of dreams and wishes
This list you choose to keep
Rather one of near misses
It keeps you from taking a leap

You consult it so frequently
Ever so neatly organized
It prevents you from being free
All its lies you have memorized

This file serves little value
Consumes valuable space
You know what you need to do
From your memory bank erase

It has become mind pollution
Leading only to defeat
One very simple solution:
Hit Ctrl Alt Delete.

June 10

Joy is what happens to us when we allow ourselves to recognize
how good things really are.
—Marianne Williamson

Seek joy. Look for it in all the corners of your life.
If you pay attention, it is not difficult to find.

Embrace joy. Hold on to it tightly. Wrap yourself within it.
Notice how all else falls away.

Know joy. You are blessed. Have you forgotten?
Look at your life. Joy is calling you home.

Share joy. It is not meant to be contained.
Be a source of joy for others. Allow it to fill all the places you go.

Be joy itself. What have you got to lose?
Perhaps sadness, worry, doubt. Seems like a good trade.

June 11

Build upon strengths, and weaknesses will gradually take care of themselves.
—Joyce C. Lock

We have come to believe it is our weakness that brings us to the brink. The truth is it is our strength. For if you were weak, you would not have made it this far.

Your strength led you to today
It will see you through tomorrow

Your strength brought you to the difficult mile
It will carry you to the next

Your strength walked you to this mountain
It will get you to the top

Your strength ran you to the wall
It will help you knock it down

Trust your strength. It has always seen you through the difficult times. It will again.

You are strong.

June 12

Happiness is a place between too little and too much.
—English proverb

Too little time
Too little gratitude
Too little grace
Too little acceptance
Too little peace
Too little kindness
Too little forgiveness
Too little understanding
Too little giving
Too little hope
Too little faith
Too little trust
HAPPINESS
Too much to do
Too much regret
Too much stress
Too much wanting
Too much blame
Too much hate
Too much anger
Too much pressure
Too much taking
Too much darkness
Too much fear
Too much doubt

Happiness. If you know where to look, you will find it.

June 13

You gain strength, courage and confidence by every experience in which you really
stop to look fear in the face. You must do the thing you think you cannot do.
—Eleanor Roosevelt

Fear is the ultimate liar
Meant to imprison you
You are meant to fly higher
So much more you can do

Fear is the worst illusion
Casts a shadow of doubt
Causing so much confusion
Time to knock fear out

Fear takes a gradual toll
As confidence it wears away
You must know in your soul
You can face anything this day

Fear has always been wrong
And you know what is true
You have always been strong
Do what you think you cannot do

Fear is but one side of the coin
Flip it over and you will see
When courage and confidence join
You become all you are meant to be.

June 14

Every person I admire who's successful and radiates an inner happiness, they
are living their truth. It's that simple. Decide what your truth is. Then live it.
—Kamal Ravikant

Dear You,

I wonder sometimes, through all the noise and confusion and trials of trying to become, I wonder if you have forgotten the truths about yourself—truths that do not change even as so much changes.

So I thought I would take this time to remind you of those truths just in case you forgot.

1. You are stronger than you give yourself credit for.

2. With all your perceived imperfections, you are still good enough.

3. You are worthy of love and happiness.

4. Your worth is not defined by a number. You are priceless.

5. You are beautiful. Everything else is a lie.

6. You can do this. Stop doubting it.

7. You always have a choice. Always.

8. You don't have to be perfect. See #2 for more details.

9. You are closer than you think. Look how far you've come.

10. You are not broken.

Now that you know your truth, it's time to act accordingly. Go live your truth.

June 15

Believe me, the reward is not so great without the struggle.
—Wilma Rudolph

The struggle is very real
Constantly it sits with me
The pain all I can feel
From it I cannot break free

The struggle is very real
The burden I carry today
At times forced to kneel
It is then I learn to pray

The struggle is very real
Questions my ability to cope
Always find a way to deal
Always, always cling to hope

The struggle is very real
Weakness consumes me
Yet strength I shall reveal
The rewards I will see

The struggle is very real
It arrives to slow my pace
Yet fire forges the steel
I shall not quit this race.

June 16

We should consider every day lost on which we have not danced at least once.
—*Friedrich Nietzsche*

Every day another chance
To hear life's symphony
To finally risk the dance
To do more than simply be

Every day another song
Played within your heart
Some wait so very long
For their dance to start

Every day the music plays
An invitation sent to you
To set your life ablaze
The flame inside lit anew

Every day time to choose:
Will you sit this one out
Fearing what you may lose
Or dance despite the doubt?

Every day a wish I send
For you to take a stance
And a song without end
That you may simply dance.

June 17

It's not how far you fall, but how high you bounce that counts.
—Zig Ziglar

At some point we all fall
Our world comes crashing in
Even if the hope is small
Once again we must begin

For it is not the fall
That defines our fate
But when you found the wall
You decided to build a gate

Yes, we will often stumble
It is all a part of the dance
No matter how far we tumble
We all get another chance

This promise you must keep
That hope cannot be trounced
It is not that you fell so deep
But that you bounced.

June 18

*Maybe everything's gotta break lose and fall apart before
we can put it back together again right.*
—Margaret McMullan

Maybe
It starts to count
When it starts to hurt

Maybe
Strength arrives
When you are weakest

Maybe
Courage is not falling
But standing every time

Maybe
Hope is just a whisper
Saying, "Try once again"

Maybe
When you're at your lowest
It is simply a reminder to look up

Maybe
As everything is stripped away
You understand all you ever had

Maybe
Faith isn't found on the mountaintop
But rather in the deepest valley

Maybe
In being completely broken apart
You recognize pieces no longer needed.

June 19

While one may encounter many defeats, one must not be defeated.
—Maya Angelou

You cannot defeat a man who does not view life in terms of wins and losses.

You cannot defeat a man who does not believe his neighbor is his greatest competition.

You cannot defeat a man who does not compare his struggles to those of another.

You cannot defeat a man who does not surrender when the road proves difficult.

You cannot defeat a man who does not fear failure.

You cannot defeat a man who does not need to be rescued.

You cannot be defeated.

June 20

You were born with potential. You were born with goodness and
trust. You were born with ideals and dreams. You were born
with greatness. You were born with wings. You are not meant for
crawling, so don't. You have wings. Learn to use them and fly.
—Rumi

I was not born with talent.

I was born with a passion, and thus my gifts have been slowly crafted.

I was not born with strength.

I was born with a beating heart, and thus my powers have been constantly nurtured.

I was not born with courage.

I was born with a fire, and thus my fears have all but been extinguished.

I was not born with grace.

I was born with a willingness to dance, and thus my steps have rarely faltered.

I was not born with greatness.

I was born with a knowing of my worth, and thus my path to success has been waiting for me to arrive.

I was not born with wings.

I was born with a belief, and thus my ability to fly has always been within me.

I was not born with foresight.

I was born with the ability to shape my life, and thus where I am headed has simply been up to me.

June 21

I'd like to take a long walk, to the edge of something.
—Arthur K. Flam

Came to the edge
Stood motionless
Hesitant. Unsure. Fearful.
Refused to jump

Came to the edge
Been here before
Filled with doubt
Turned and walked away

Came to the edge
Unable to simply leap
Feared not the jump
But rather the fall

Came to the edge
Took the leap
Trusted the landing
And my ability to fly

June 22

What we are waiting for is not as important as what happens
to us while we are waiting. Trust the process.
—Mandy Hale

I crawled long before I walked.
Struggled
To find my footing.

I walked long before I ran
Teetered
On the brink of falling.

I ran long before I found my wings.
Slowly
Building strength for the jump.

I leapt long before I could soar.
Trusting
I was always meant to fly.

Crawl.
Walk.
Run.
Leap.
Fly.

This is the evolution of flight.

It is a process.
Trust the process.
Trust yourself.

June 23

If I've never stepped outside the role that's been assigned to me since birth, I've never tested myself. I've been too afraid of others' opinions, I think. I've been a coward.
—Elizabeth Hoyt

You will never know if you can fly

If you never test your wings.

You will never know how much you can achieve

If you never test your limits.

You will never know the heights you can reach

If you never test your comfort zone.

You will never know what exists past the darkness

If you never test your light.

You will never know what is beyond the horizon

If you never test your fears.

This is only a test.

It is not an actual emergency.

You can do this.

June 24

*What lies behind us and what lies before us are tiny
matters compared to what lies within us.*
—Ralph Waldo Emerson

The past got you here.

The future anxiously awaits your arrival.

The present knows what lies within you.

Strength of your convictions.

Truth from lessons learned.

Unwavering belief.

Toughness.

Kindness.

Awesomeness.

A fire burning bright.

Inner beauty and light.

Unquenchable desire.

Hopes, dreams, ambitions.

A good and gentle heart.

What lies inside you has always been enough.

June 25

The very least you can do in your life is figure out what you hope for. And the most you can do is live inside that hope. Not admire it from a distance but live right in it, under its roof.
—Barbara Kingsolver

Hope got me up this day.
She is my alarm clock.

Hope sits with me this morning.
She is my comfort.

Hope walks alongside me.
She is my constant companion.

Hope lifts me when I fall.
She is my strength.

Hope protects me from my storms.
She is my safe harbor.

Hope sees me through the darkness.
She is my lighthouse.

Hope will get me where I am going.
She is my compass.

There is a truth I know.
With hope, I can endure all.
With hope, I am completely alive.

Have hope.

June 26

The more you know who you are, and what you
want, the less you let things upset you.
—Stephanie Perkins

You are better.
Rise above.

You are strong.
Be gentle in word and action.

You are kind.
Show compassion.

You have time.
Practice patience.

You are enough.
Give freely.

You are grand.
Leave no room for pettiness.

You are brave.
Show courage.

You are gifted.
Share your talents.

You are light.
Shine the way.

You are the answer.
Solve the problem.

Remember who you are.
Remember what you want.
Respond in a way that honors you.

June 27

You are not a drop in the ocean, you are the entire ocean in a drop.
—Rumi

What if?

What if, just for today, you understood your immense power and vastness?

How would that change what you believed you could accomplish?

What if, just for today, you knew what an agent of change and calming influence you are?

How would that change how you handled the struggles of the day?

What if, just for today, you realized your incredible beauty and depth?

How would that change how you view yourself?

What if, just for today, you saw yourself as a miracle?

How would that change how you allowed others to treat you and how you treat yourself?

Powerful and vast.

Capable of change.

Calm.

Beautiful and deep.

A miracle.

What if, just for today, you simply believed?

June 28

You can't reach for anything new if your hands are still full of yesterday's junk.
—Louise Smith

I hope you wake with empty hands
If you must fill them, be it with the hands of one in need

I hope you rinse your hands clean
If they must be soiled, let it be from the hard work of chasing a dream

I hope your hands are not wrought with sadness
If they must come together, let it be in prayer for another

I hope your hands are never thrown up in frustration
If they must be lifted, let it be to feel the beating of your heart

I hope your hands finally let go
If you must hold on, let it be faith you cling to

I hope your hands know the touch of a loved one
If you must reach out, let it be for those who always care

I hope for you all good things.

June 29

You are enough not because you did or said or thought or bought or became or created something special, but because you always were.
—Liv Lane

I went looking for you in all the wrong places
Into their eyes I gazed and in so many other faces
Today I looked with my heart, and who should I see?
You, my beautiful reflection, looking right back at me

I searched for you for so very long
No longer wanting to be weak, I hoped to be strong
I rummaged the broken pieces scattered around
Deep inside me, my strength, you were found

I called out to you in the distance, the dark
I needed you to desperately light a spark
The storm it blows, the fire it does tame
Yet, my soul, you were an eternal flame

I wondered aloud how much value you truly hold
Silently I thought you were easily sold
You are my worth, and now I confess
You are rare and priceless

You are beauty, strength, light, and worth.
You are more than enough.
You always have been.

June 30

Think not that humility is weakness; it shall supply the marrow of strength to thy bones. Stoop and conquer; bow thyself and become invincible.
—*Charles Spurgeon*

At times been made to bow
Hard times just won't relent
Found a way somehow
To rise from being bent

At times been made to bow
A hard road becoming longer
Accept where I am right now
Know I am becoming stronger

At times been made to bow
Forced to take a little rest
Gathering courage in the now
Again I shall pass this test

At times been made to bow
Life tried to steal my victory
But I will not surrender now
There is no quit in me

Been made to bow repeatedly
I bowed, but never did I fall
If you look closely, you will see
This bow 'tis merely my curtain call.

July 1

Every day brings with it the promise of a new beginning.
—Katrina Mayer

Keep the promises made to yourself
For too long they have remained on the shelf
Anything and everything is possible this day
When you believe there is always a way

Let your promises be bold and spoken
From this day forth let none be broken
Make a promise to be a much happier you
So let it be spoken, so let it be true

Promise to allow yourself some fun
See the miracles, walk in the sun
Let yourself heal a promise made to your heart
Let this be the day you give it a start

Promise to never, ever quit
Do not doubt you can do it
Get up and get on your way
Choose to see the possibilities of this day

Promise to walk tall and proud
Dance your song and sing out loud
With arms wide open, embrace the day
"I promise," the words you say.

July 2

Hope is not a strategy, luck is not a factor, fear is not an option.
—James Cameron

Hope is that which gives us reason
To see the beauty in every season
We must always keep hope within our heart
Hope keeps us from falling apart

Yet hope is simply the light
It needs a goal to keep it burning bright
Have a dream and a plan to achieve
Hope then makes it easy to believe

Luck has no real role in your life
It doesn't cause joy or sorrow, blessings or strife
Luck, good or bad, is not cast upon you
It does not decide what you are able to do

You are too gifted and too able
To need luck to sit at your table
Have belief in yourself and you will see
Just how "lucky" you will be

Fear is such a curious beast
Once inside our minds, it has a feast
Devouring that which we know is true
Fear is a liar, it does not believe in you

Fear is the bully in the schoolyard
Overcoming it is sometimes hard
But fear is not welcome in this place
Stand up to it, punch it in the face

Have hope but have a plan
Wish others good luck but make your own
Look fear in the eye but then tell it good-bye

July 3

We as human beings have this amazing capacity to be reborn at breakfast every day and say, "This is a day. Who will I be?"
—Jack Kornfield

Today, I will strive to be
The person living inside of me
The one capable of forgiveness
Give a little more, take a little less

Today, I hope I am being
More than the world is seeing
One who can simply be strong
Who I was meant to be all along

Today, I choose to be
The very best of me
Finally unleashed from yesterday
Finally able to get out of my own way

Today, I am better than before
Picked myself up off the floor
Arms wide open, I greet the day
Allowing goodness to come my way

Today, I remain completely me
For I know who I want to be
To get here has been rough
I finally believe I am good enough

With this knowing, forward I go
Still so much I can grow
Yet today I am at peace
Doubting myself can finally cease

So as I begin this new day
Let my spoken diary say
I found out who I will be
Simply, beautifully me.

July 4

Our greatest weakness lies in giving up.
—Thomas A. Edison

Weakness eventually finds us all
Before us waits our personal wall
Some will choose to simply give up
Never to sip from the golden cup

Weakness, perhaps a demon from the past
Or a new monster approaching fast
Weakness will seek you out
It preys on fear, feasts on doubt

Weakness wants to drive you to your knees
It cares not about your pleas
Weakness wants for you to crawl
It stands in silence to watch you fall

It is when you feel most weak
Into your heart you must peek
What weakness failed to know all along
Is that you are simply too strong

Weakness will say, "You want to quit"
Choose not to listen to it
Call it stubbornness, pride, or guts
You will not give up, no ifs, ands, or buts

When weakness comes knocking at your door
Invite it in then slam it to the floor
There is no longer room for it here
The weakness you no longer fear

For what we must realize
Perhaps see with our very eyes
The weakness will only reveal
Our resolve, our courage, our steel.

July 5

If you never attempt the ascent, you'll never know the
thrill of swooshing down the other side.
—Unknown

Came to the mountain
Destined to fail, I could not win
The climb would be too great
To know the other side not my fate
Stood so long at the bottom of that hill
Longing for the thrill
To know what was on the other side
The climb too steep, so I never tried

May as well have been a great crevasse
Either way, I could not pass
Never would I reach the top
Before I began, I would always stop
Came up with every excuse
Wore them like a hangman's noose
My excuses began to define me
Clung to them like a prized trophy

Finally got tired of standing still
Decided to go and conquer that hill
No path to keep me on track
Many times kept sliding back
At times afraid of the height
Other times weary of the fight
Each day, climbed a bit longer
Each day, grew a bit stronger

Not always sure where to go
What awaited I did not know
Just knew it was time to start
On this journey of the heart
So go and face your hill
Go and find your thrill
But know that somebody lied
Glory not found on the other side

If you simply choose to go
You will come to finally know
It's not about the other side
It's that you finally tried.

July 6

It's not hard to make decisions when you know what your values are.
—Roy Disney

My challenge every single day
Be better in all I do, all I say
Values held close I try to live
Give the best I have to give

Speak the truth as if my words were gold
Being kind never grows old
Reach out to help another
Treat a stranger as if a brother

Walk as if I am someone's hero
Light the way for others to go
Help others to walk along
Until they can learn to walk strong

Allow others to simply be
Hold no one back, including me
Change the way someone looks at today
Because I merely passed by their way

Be the change I want to see
For in valuing you, I honor me
A new day changes not what's true
I know and live what I value.

July 7

I guess everyone has a bird urge when they look down heights, a desire to jump,
without wing or buoyant sail. Fear of heights is fear of a desire to jump.
– Amruta Patil

You stood at the very edge of healing
Fear made you feel broken
And so you dared not jump
Never knowing you are permitted
To finally allow yourself to be OK

You stood at the very edge of change
Fear made you cling to the past
And so you dared not jump
Never knowing letting loose that chain
Will allow you to truly soar.

You stood at the very edge of magic
Fear made the net invisible
And so you dared not jump
Never knowing the magic occurs
When you believe you will be caught.

You stood at the very edge of love
Fear made you question it
And so you dared not jump
Never knowing your heart knows
This love was the answer you sought.

You stand at the very edge of your life.
Something amazing awaits
Just beyond the edge of fear
Healing. Change. Magic. Love.
Dare to jump.

July 8

Don't sweat the small stuff...and it's all small stuff.
—Richard Carlson

If I am to sweat, it shall not be over the small stuff.

The pettiness of that which will not matter come day's end.

The minor details soon lost, for they truly mattered not.

Effort focused there does not honor the size of my dreams.

If I am to sweat, it shall not be over what I cannot change or control.

The actions, attitudes, and words of others.

My yesterdays and my tomorrows.

Energy spent there is but wasted.

If I am to sweat, it shall not be out of fear.

Fear produces little movement, little change, little opportunity for growth.

Time given my fears is time not well spent.

If I am to sweat, it shall be in pursuit of a dream.

It shall be for the hard work of changing old habits.

It shall be for finding the courage to take the leap.

July 9

The only permission, the only validation, and the only opinion that matters in our quest for greatness is our own.
—Steve Maraboli

Give yourself permission to be great
The haters will always hate
Does not matter what they think
It's up to you to swim or sink

Give yourself permission to arise from the crowd
Doubters' voices will seem so loud
Does not matter what they think
When you are standing at the brink

Greatness is your truth and destiny
No matter what others think they see
What matters related to what you achieve
Is that which you most believe

Others may not want to see you win
But greatness comes from within
So let them go ahead and talk
Words have no power over your walk

So put your greatness on display
In all you do and all you say
Other voices will fall silent
It is greatness for which you're meant

And if you wonder where to start
Simply look inside your heart
If you search, you need not roam very far
You are great just as you are.

July 10

If we will be quiet and ready enough, we shall find compensation
in every disappointment.
—Henry David Thoreau

Life and I had another little chat.

Life: I made the struggles of yesterday so great you will have no strength for today.

Me: Sorry to disappoint you; yesterday's struggles only made me stronger.

Life: I will throw so much at you today, you will have no time to do what you want or need to do.

Me: Sorry to disappoint you; I have my priorities in order, and I have plenty of time.

Life: I will fill this day will stresses, excuses, and challenges to keep you from achieving what you set out to accomplish.

Me: Sorry to disappoint you; stress comes from a lack of acceptance. I'm good where I'm at. Excuses do not trump my discipline. Challenges are merely opportunities to grow.

Life: Do I disappoint you?

Me: No matter how hard you try, you couldn't. I love the life I'm living.

July 11

You get in life what you have the courage to ask for.
—Oprah Winfrey

Questions left unasked are never responded to.
So ask.

Prayers never said are never answered.
So pray.

Dreams never chased are never caught.
So go in pursuit.

Wishes never made are never granted.
So wish.

It takes courage to ask.

Faith to pray.

Hope to dream.

Belief to wish.

May you find these within you.

July 12

The price tag that you put on your soul will determine the
people and circumstances in which you find yourself.
—Shannon L. Alder

I awoke to thoughts of you
Wondering if you truly knew
Of your very special value.
To your worth are you true?

Can you simply comprehend
You have a worth without end?
When this knowing does arrive
Your very soul shall finally thrive

No one can give you this
It's your very own self kiss
You are already valuable
Write it so it's indelible

Allow the knowing to start
Your worth is from the heart
It cannot be dulled or erased
By the trials you have faced

One constant remains true
Priceless is the value of you
You cannot be bought or sold
Yours is a soul of pure gold

Your soul now longing to be led
By a new message in your head
You are so very worthy
Of all the best that can be.

July 13

Your life will fly by, so make sure you're the pilot.
—Rob Liano

This is your very own life
Not up to friends, husband, or wife
You are the one who gets to choose
And that is the very best news

You're the driver of your bus
Where you go, not up to us
Foot off the brake, move those wheels
Before another day this life steals

You're the singer of your song
A melody straight from the heart
So this day belt it out loud
Only you can sing your part

You are your own lifeguard
This isn't really hard
Dare to jump into the wave
Your own lifetime to save

You're the runner of your race
No one else can set your pace
Go running toward your dreams
Let them not come apart at the seams

You are the author of your story
What will your next chapter be?
Let every word written come to say
You did not waste another day.

July 14

It is always so simple, and so complicating, to accept an apology.
—Michael Chabon

You never offered an apology
For all the wrongs done to me
Many mistakes *you* did make
Time to apologize *you* did not take

"I am sorry" was never heard
Waited so long but not a word
An apology was much needed
To *you*, I begged and pleaded

How could *you* not clearly see
How much *you* were hurting me?
All the betrayal and all the lies
The tears *you* brought to my eyes

You said I was unworthy
Proclaimed it a truth about me
In me, *you* seemed ashamed
You were wrong, but I was blamed

You could not see my value
You only wanted someone new
I had come to regret and fear
"I am sorry" I would never hear

Before me breaks a new day
New words that I can say
For I have come to realize
I don't need *you* to apologize

For *you* were *me* all along
To myself was doing wrong
You were merely my echo
A voice I now let go

I completely forgive me
Of my own mistakes now free
"I am sorry" finally came
I simply added my own name.

July 15

Instead of either/or, I discovered a whole world of and.
—Gloria Steinem

Either I could wonder what is on the other side of my wall

Or I could simply tear it down

Either I could wonder what is on the other side of my darkness

Or I could become a lighthouse

Either I could wonder what is on the other side of my fears

Or I could find the courage to take the leap

Either I could wonder what is on the other side of my today

Or I could set a course for my tomorrows

Either I could wonder what is on the other side of my dreams

Or I could construct my home there

If you wonder the choice I made

I would simply reply, "I stopped wondering."

July 16

Some journeys can only be traveled alone.
—Ken Poirot

Again I must take to the road
As I endlessly roam
Burdened with a heavy load
Taking the long way home

Beside me an empty seat
For the journey is my own
Traveled in victory or defeat
I am forced to go it alone

If I could take a friend
Hope would go with me
One day the journey to end
That I may finally be

If I could hold a hand
Kindness I would embrace
For no matter where I land
I would arrive with grace

If I could travel with one key
Forgiveness kept in my pocket
For every gate put before me
I could easily unlock it

If I could share the road
Love I would take with me
For every toll ever owed
I would have the currency

Wish me well as I go
For I must be on my way
There is something I know
One day, I will be OK

Hope and kindness by my side
And with love and forgiveness
This won't be such a difficult ride
For the burden shall be much less.

July 17

*I wanted a perfect ending. Now I've learned, the hard way, that some poems
don't rhyme, and some stories don't have a clear beginning, middle, and end.
Life is about not knowing, having to change, taking the moment and making the
best of it, without knowing what's going to happen next. Delicious ambiguity.*
—*Gilda Radner*

Life is an awkward dance
To music hard to hear
Always another chance
To dance without fear

Life is a message being sent
Verses of the aching
Lines of how I've bent
But never am I breaking

Life is an ebb and flowing
Lost and adrift at sea
In a search for knowing
Of all I am supposed to be

Life is an unopened door
Something waits for me
Beyond it so much more
If I'm willing to turn the key

Life is a long-distance run
On a difficult trail
Yet the race will be won
By starting, I cannot fail

Life is an amazing journey
Allowing me to roam
To grow, learn, and be
Then bringing me home.

July 18

Do one thing every day that scares you.
—*Eleanor Roosevelt*

Go ahead, be afraid
Then do it anyway
It's where dreams are made
Believe, leap, pray

Fears are not meant to stop you
They simply play a part
For all they are meant to do
Is let you feel your beating heart

Facing fear is what life's all about
To overcome, to accomplish
That which you once did doubt
For you, this is my wish

We all know what it's like
To have our fears take hold
Tell them to take a hike
Time to break the mold

If it scares you, give it a try
You'll never truly know
If you have wings to fly
If to the edge you never go.

July 19

The vision may be the destination but the journey began with a past which will stay connected whatever the sages may say against it—there is always a hyperlink.
—Amit Abraham

Thank you.

For every tear shed
And the deep waters tread

For all the lessons learned
And beautiful scars earned

For that which I lost
And learning all it cost

For sadness and regret
And memories never to forget

For the loves I have known
And the beauty I've been shown

For teaching what I must know
And finally letting me go

These my thanks to yesterday
So grateful you led me to today.

July 20

Your mind, it will trick you, but your heart, it will not.
—Nikki Rowe

My brain and my heart are not always on the same page.

Choosing the right one to follow, in that moment, is where my life unfolds.

My brain rarely sleeps, for it cannot filter out the noise. It captures everything. The minor details and grand illusions. A gift and a burden. Its conversation with me is constant.

My heart is always vulnerable, for it is open and exposed. It feels everything. The joys and sufferings of others. A gift and a burden. Its conversation with me is constant.

Sometimes those conversations collided.

My brain said, "Do not do it."
My heart said, "Go ahead—give it a try."

My brain said, "Stay in control."
My heart said, "Stop playing it safe."

My brain said, "You could get hurt."
My heart said, "Regret is unimaginable pain."

My brain said, "Consider the risks."
My heart said, "Imagine the rewards."

My brain said, "Think it through."
My heart said, "Allow yourself to feel."

I went with my brain. It won out.

My heart is a bit heavy. It knows what was lost.

My brain rarely sleeps. My heart is always vulnerable.

A gift and a burden.

July 21

If you ask me what I came into this life to do, I will tell you: I came to live out loud.
—Emile Zola

A friend asked of me, "What does it look like for you to go get today?"

And so I thought I would attempt to paint that picture.

First, if the truth be told, it has very little to do with my running or training. Although that is obviously a part of it, for it helps to complete me.

But more, it is about taking the day and absorbing all the wonders it holds. The miracles. The beauty. The dreams. The messages.

Being more present with those around me. Listening more intently. Embracing them where they are. Acknowledging their importance in my day. Being gentle with their humanness.

Finding my gratitude in the small pieces of my day. In those parts so easily overlooked or taken for granted. Recognizing and receiving the gifts placed before me.

Pushing myself to learn something new. To personally grow. To challenge my own limited thinking and belief system. To embrace the fullness of the life I have been given.

Gathering the moments instead of gathering things. For longer walks. For more meaningful talks. For more laughter. For truly living instead of simply existing.

Finding the spaces in my day where there should be joy instead of unhappiness. Quiet where there is noise. Peace where there is unrest. Gratitude where there is want.

Taking time to pursue passions. To give to others. To refill my curiosity. To explore the deepest corners of me. To live and dream with arms and eyes and heart wide open.

July 22

It does not take much strength to do things, but it requires
a great deal of strength to decide what to do.
—Elbert Hubbard

I did not know where the road would lead me.

I simply decided to appreciate the view it afforded me.

And I did not feel so lost.

I did not know how far I would have to travel.

I simply decided to enjoy taking the long way home.

And I grew to know patience.

I did not know the path would be filled with so many obstacles.

I simply decided to look at them as opportunities.

And I began to understand what it means to grow.

I did not know the journey would be so long.

I simply decided to take it one step at a time.

And I know with each step, I am that much closer to home.

I did not know what would be my destiny.

I simply decided to chase my dreams.

And I have no regrets.

Looking back, I realize when it came to my life, I simply decided how I would live it.

July 23

The ache for home lives in all of us. The safe place where
we can go as we are and not be questioned.
—Maya Angelou

Aching for home. A somewhere.

Where my frailties are seen as strengths.

Where my scars are seen as beauty marks.

Where my oddities are seen as normal.

Aching for home. A someone.

Someone to see the perfection beyond my faults.

Someone to see the courage beyond my fears.

Someone to see the best of me beyond my worst.

Aching for home. A time.

When I will feel comfortable in my own skin.

When I will believe in myself.

When I will stop aching.

The somewhere: this place I stand.

The someone: myself.

The time: has come.

For when I show up as me and truly honor and cherish who I am, I will finally be home.

The aching can end.

July 24

When within yourself you find the road, the right road will open.
– Dejan Stanjanovic

Dear Life,

I want to go on a road trip. Just you and I. Windows down. Radio blaring. Warm breeze blowing. Seat belts buckled. For this won't be your Sunday drive.

I want to go on a road trip. Just you and I. No particular place to go. Back roads. Broken roads. Roads uncharted. For there is not always a map to a dream.

I want to go on a road trip. Just you and I. We will talk. Of dreams and hopes. Of things small and grand. And oh, how we will sing. Songs we know by heart. Lyrics we thought time had erased.

I want to go on a road trip. Just you and I. So many memories to be chased. From being lost to all we shall find. From moonlit mornings to star-kissed nights and the magic in between. From the mysteries that await to the truths we shall learn.

I want to go on a road trip. Just you and I. For you are the road within me, and you shall lead me where I am to be. To that place where I can finally exhale. To that holy place where light and love exist. To that place called home.

I want to go on a road trip. Just you and I.

Love, Me

July 25

There's nothing more inspiring than the complexity
and beauty of the human heart.
—Cynthia Hand

To hold hope in your heart is to trust the light will appear beyond the darkness.

To hold hope in your heart is to believe in the promises you made to yourself.

To hold hope in your heart is to have faith in all that cannot yet be seen.

To hold hope in your heart is to find peace.

To hold peace in your heart is to accept that where you are is right where you are meant to be.

To hold peace in your heart is to let go of the fears you desperately cling to.

To hold peace in your heart is count the blessings and gifts in your life.

To hold peace in your heart is to find strength.

To hold strength in your heart is to realize you are not broken.

To hold strength in your heart is to finally forgive yourself.

To hold strength in your heart is to have the courage to unconditionally love yourself.

To hold strength in your heart is to find peace.

Hope. Peace. Strength.

All you hold in your heart, you will find at hand.

July 26

If you dare nothing, then when the day is over, nothing is all you have gained.
—Neil Gaiman

I dare you to fail miserably
To let go of the outcome
Whatever will be will be
For in the trying you become

I dare you to simply let go
Loosen your stranglehold
Answers you need not know
In the letting go, they unfold

I dare you to just be OK
To not sweat the small stuff
Whatever life sends your way
You've always been strong enough

I dare you to believe in you
To put aside your doubt
No longer fear what is true
Let the real you come out

I dare you to give yourself a break
Your own self forgive
Not fret over every mistake
Let yourself truly live

I dare you to live life full force
To go and get today
Upon it set a new course
Then go and be on your way.

July 27

Happiness is the consequence of personal effort. You must fight for it, strive for it, insist upon it.
—Rev. Run

Happiness is...

A towel straight from the dryer

The smell of rain and then seeing the rainbow

The sound of children's laughter

A new pair of shoes

Dancing in your living room

Finding cash in your pocket

Windows down, moon roof open

Jeans day at work

An unexpected but needed hug

Lemonade with a friend

Your favorite song on the radio

A blanket, a fire, a good book

The sound of your coffee maker

A wagging tail and warm snuggles

Coming home after a long day

Happiness is all around us,

Found in the small details of your day.

You must be willing to look for it and then be able to recognize it.

Wishing you a day filled with little bits of happiness.

July 28

Spread your love everywhere you go.
—*Mother Teresa*

Today I will...

Love who I am
Love what I am
Love where I am

Today I will...

Love my body
Love myself
Love my imperfections

Today I will...

Love my friends
Love my doubters
Love my neighbors

Today I will...

Love myself better
Love myself enough
Love myself completely

Today I will...

Love my struggles
Love my journey
Love my life

Today I will be a source of love and light.
No one shall pass through me without being left better for it.
Spread your love.

July 29

Today expect something good to happen to you no matter what occurred yesterday. Realize the past no longer holds you captive. It can only continue to hurt you if you hold on to it. Let the past go.
A simply abundant world awaits.
—Sarah Ban Breathnach

This letter arrived for you today.

Dear _____,

Please let me go. I am no longer serving any useful purpose.
My value to you has expired.

Please let me go. I am only going to pull you under.
My presence has become an anchor.

Please let me go. I am not the direction you are heading.
My path is now closed to through traffic.

Please let me go. I am unable to show you the way forward.
My compass will only lead you astray.

Please let me go. I am imposing hefty baggage fees.
My burdens you need not carry.

Please let me go. I am distorting how you view yourself.
My lens no longer reflects who you are.

Please let me go.

Love,

Yesterday

July 30

Smile, breathe, and go slowly.
—Thich Nhat Hanh

Go forth with a smile
Tears are not meant to last
You have survived the trial
The rains have all but passed

Find the many reasons
To offer a smile today
Like the passing seasons
Hope again comes your way

Go forth and breathe
Slow, purposeful, and deep
Let not anger seethe
It serves no purpose to keep

Inhale that which you seek
Exhale all doubt and fear
Exhale when you are weak
Inhale deep, strength is here

Go forth slowly
Do not hasten as you go
Allow things just to be
All answers you need not know

You will find your way
But life is about the journey
So slow down today
Allow yourself to simply be.

July 31

Just for today, smile a little more. Just for today, ask someone how he or she is really doing. Just for today, remember, while some may have it better than you do, there are others whom definitely have it worse than you! Just for today, just let go, just for today...
—James A. Murphy

Today, like the next mile ahead of me, simply waits to see what I shall bring to it.
It is not difficult, it does not set the tone, it has no expectations.

Today, like the next mile ahead of me, simply waits to find out what exists inside of me.
It does not determine that, it is not a test, it cannot define me.

Today, like the next mile ahead of me, simply waits for me to decide how I shall move through it.
It has no power to decide that, it cannot change my stride, it does not set my pace.

Today, like the next mile ahead of me, simply waits for me to arrive.
It cares not about my excuses, it asks no questions, it holds no judgments.

Today is the next mile.

I simply choose to enjoy the view.

I simply choose to take my time.

I simply choose to feel strong.

I simply choose to smile through it.

I simply choose to find my breath.

I simply choose to bring my best to it.

For today, like the next mile, is all I know.

August 1

Stop being scared of failing. Be scared of not trying.
—Karen Salmansohn

Between existing and living, a precipice
Very few dare to risk the leap
Thus, so much will they miss
A fear in their hearts they keep

For a fear of trying
Or a fear of defeat
Small pieces begin dying
True destiny we do not meet

A vision in our eyes
Of what we want to be
But fear does paralyze
Our true selves we never see

If we can just stand still
We will never hurt or lose
But dreams we slowly kill
When this is what we choose

Too often we fear the falling
Never knowing we have wings
We miss our true calling
To do simply amazing things

Times there will be a setback
Times you will know heartache
Simply get back on track
You are too strong to break

Many times you may fail
Yet you are not a failure
Nor are you weak or frail
You found strength to endure.

August 2

Two roads diverged in the wood, and I took the one less traveled by, and that has made all the difference.
—Robert Frost

I've been taking the long way home
On a road that never seems to end
Perhaps I've been made to roam
In search of a life just beyond the bend

Alone I have traveled this road
Where it leads I cannot always see
Down the road many tolls have been owed
The price paid for becoming me

This road allows for little rest
My steps often weary and slow
For I have failed many a test
And yet along this road I still go

In the distance a signpost ahead
Come to know what it shall say
Its words I no longer dread
You are not home, you must not stay

Along this road are all my stories
Traveled with tears and smiles
My many losses and few glories
A life defined in the difficult miles

If perhaps given another chance
I would not choose any different
I would not chance my stance
This the road for which I was meant.

August 3

Nobody is superior, nobody is inferior, but nobody is equal either.
People are simply unique, incomparable. You are you, I am I.
—Osho

If you are wanting to change the world,

Simply be you.

Your being authentic alters every corner of your world.

If you are looking for a light in the world,

Simply be you.

Your smile, your kindness, your presence light the way for others.

If you are seeking truth in the world,

Simply be you.

Nothing speaks with greater clarity than when you show up as you.

If you are wishing for peace in the world,

Simply be you.

When you no longer attempt to conform to another's ideal of you, peace reigns.

If you are searching for beauty in the world,

Simply be you.

No greater beauty exists than when we quietly, completely, and confidently love ourselves.

Whatever it is you are after this day, it can be found if you will simply be you.

August 4

Believe on Monday, the way you believed on Sunday.
—Rita Schiano

I am a believer. That may or may not sit well with others.

Some may suggest I do not understand or that I pretend that everything is wonderful.

They would be incorrect. Truth is, I simply believe. And that belief does not waver based on the day of the week, my current mood, or the actions of others.

I believe:

1. In the power of the human spirit to rise above its current condition

2. In forgiveness, happiness, having faith, honesty, paying it forward

3. In the power of positive thought

4. Life isn't always easy, but it is always good, beautiful, and amazing

5. Greatness is possible; that anything is possible

6. Miracles happen

7. Having a quiet, humble, steady belief in yourself is vital to success

8. In my ability to change my small corner of the world

9. I am worthy, capable, good enough, valuable, loved

10. Light trumps darkness, faith conquers fear, love defeats hate…every single time

And with this belief, I walk with my head held up, a smile on my face, confidently in the direction of my dreams.

August 5

You only live once, but if you do it right, once is enough.
—Mae West

Life is about doing.
Living
Breathing
Flying
Exploring
Loving
Dancing
Trying
Learning
Doing

Life is about being.
Happy
Kind
Forgiving
Understanding
Loving
Patient
Gentle
Wise
True
Being

Life is about becoming.
Strong
Real
Genuine
You
Becoming

Life is about what you will simply choose with your next breath, thought, word, action.

August 6

All we are is a bunch of dozy people in the process of waking up.
All we really need to do is try gently to be open to continuing that process.
—Jay Woodman

Did you wake up completely in love with your life?
Embracing your blessings, as well as your strife
Your blessings make it easy to move along
Your strife is what makes you truly strong.

Did you wake up completely in love with who you are?
Loving your beauty and each and every scar
Your beauty says you have an inner light
Your scars say you've survived the fight.

Did you wake up completely at peace with today?
Looking forward to tomorrow, letting go of yesterday
Your yesterday has set you free
Your tomorrow a dream ready to be

Did you wake up completely willing to do what it may take?
New steps to dance, old habits to break
New steps forward without fear
Old habits let go without a tear

Did you wake up completely appreciating where you are?
Places to go, yet realizing you've come so far
You may not be where you want to be
Yet where you stand, be truly happy.

My wish for you this day and for your tomorrows is that you did.

August 7

Wherever the bird with no feet flew, she found trees with no limbs.
—Audre Lorde

You flitter from place to place
Hoping somewhere to land
Memories wanting to erase
Pain you can no longer stand

Away you continue to fly
You've learned to take flight
So no one can see you cry
Easier to give up than to fight

Your wings growing weary
For how long you search
Skies ahead dark and dreary
Shadows hide your perch

So fly if you feel you must
In search of your place to land
Not your wings you need trust
You must finally take a stand

Grant permission to just be
Let go of that which you fear
Loving yourself sets you free
And the limb will finally appear.

August 8

There is nothing more beautiful than seeing a person being themselves.
Imagine going through your day being unapologetically you.
—Steve Maraboli

1. So much in life is not what you do but the attitude you take toward what you do, which matters most.

2. As you seek to give of your gifts, so much shall be returned to you.

3. You are not always chosen to lead, but in serving others, you become a leader.

4. When you allow love to guide your actions, you will know joy.

5. Your smile sends a beautiful message to the world. The world needs such a message.

6. You have been given this life and a choice of how you shall spend it. Choose to dance.

7. If you are not having fun, you are probably doing it wrong.

8. Wherever you go, carry your light. Not so others can see you, but so you may shine it upon them.

9. Raise your words but never your voice.

10. Above all, be you. For therein lies freedom.

August 9

Those who overcome great challenges will be changed, and often in unexpected ways. For our struggles enter our lives as unwelcome guests, but they bring valuable gifts. And once the pain subsides, the gifts remain. These gifts are life's true treasures, bought at great price, but cannot be acquired in any other way.
—Steve Goodier

Every day, we are each presented the same three gifts. Yet I wonder if we receive them as the treasures they truly are.

Or do we merely set them aside, waiting and wishing for something more, different, better?

Never realizing these gifts hold all we shall ever need.

The gifts I speak of, granted every single day: choices, chances, challenges.

Each day, I have the choice to do, become, and be all that I decide for myself.
And with such choice comes power and freedom.

Each day, I am afforded the chance to change anything that is not serving my greater good. I do not have to settle. And, thus, growth and progress are always available to me.

Each day, I am faced with challenges. Often I overlook this as a gift. Yet it may be the greatest gift handed to me. For in accepting my challenges, I become stronger, more resilient, and a better version of myself.

Choices, chances, challenges.
These gifts you are given today.
Receive them with arms and heart wide open.

August 10

You are unfolding with profound purpose; your purpose is revealing you,
to yourself.
—Bryant McGill

Dear You,

I reflected on what I am witnessing about you and wanted to sit and write you a letter.

Have you stopped recently to appreciate how truly remarkable you are? To fully embrace just how special and amazing you are? I am learning lessons about you, and they humble me.

I am witnessing as you push your body to new limits, to new places beyond your threshold, and I marvel.

Despite all the things you do not like about it, your perceived imperfections and flaws, your wishing you could make it different, it is capable of producing miracles. Your body is a remarkable work of art, a thing of beauty, an incredible machine. Embrace it, talk gently to it, learn to truly love it.

I am witnessing as you push through trials and pain, setbacks and heartache, and I am amazed by your spirit and strength.

Despite the odds and difficulties, challenges and obstacles, you refuse to quit. You continue to rise and try again. Your spirit is powerful beyond measure. You are stronger than you know. Give yourself credit, breathe deep, begin again; it is what you know to do.

I am witnessing as you shine your light on others, and I bask in its brilliant glow. You are a gift, a wonder in the world, you make a difference, and you change lives.

Do not shy away from your own light. Acknowledge how special you are; let that light shine on yourself so you can see all the beauty and wonder we see in you.

I am witnessing as you continue to chase your dreams, as you set new goals, as you pursue the horizon, and I am inspired.

Don't ever give up on your dreams. Have faith, keep hope, walk toward it every day, know they are achievable. You inspire so many, you give hope to others, you help us reach our dreams.

You are beautiful, strong, a brilliant light, a keeper of dreams. You are a very special gift. When you gently unfold, we are all rewarded.

May you walk this day knowing how truly remarkable and special you are. I have been witness, and I know.

August 11

What is the point of being alive if you don't at least try to do something remarkable?
—John Green

Too often we misunderstand the idea of greatness, of being remarkable. For it isn't really a grand spectacle. It comes in a steadfast commitment to doing small things that will ultimately lead to amazing changes. So today, may you be remarkably:

Kind

Loving

Giving

Happy

Healthy

Gentle

Outgoing

Helpful

Pleasant

Open

Peaceful

Accepting

Willing

Calm

Steady

You.

For in doing the remarkable, anything is possible.

August 12

You need to let the little things that would ordinarily bore you suddenly thrill you.
—Andy Warhol

If I could buy you a gift, I would purchase just a little something.
Just a little time, a little quiet, a little peace, a little understanding.

Time to spend with one you love.
Quiet to hear your heart's whisper.
Peace of mind when you are burdened.
Understanding of your beautiful gifts.

If I could make a wish come true for you, I would make just a little wish.
Just a little love, a little dream, a little light, a little knowing.

Love of yourself.
Dreams you see with eyes open.
Light to keep away the darkness.
Knowing that something wonderful awaits.

If I could give you all things, I would give you just a little.
Just a little happiness, a little sunshine, a little space, a little hope.

Happiness you carry always.
Sunshine to warm your path.
Space to find yourself.
Hope you can cling to.

Just a little can make everything better.
Just a little can bring us more fully alive.
Just a little is all it really takes.

Today, may you have just a little.
And in that, you just may have everything.

August 13

Happiness is not something ready-made. It comes from your own actions.
—*Dalai Lama XIV*

Watch the sunrise
Watch an old movie
Watch children play

Gaze at the stars
Gaze out the window
Gaze into love's eyes

Listen to your favorite song
Listen to nature
Listen to your heart

Snuggle your children
Snuggle your puppy
Snuggle your soul

Laugh until you cry
Laugh until you snort
Laugh some more

Take a nap
Take a walk
Take time for you

Walk along the beach
Walk along the river
Walk a new path

Get dressed up
Get outside
Get a run in

Call a friend
Call your mom
Call in healthy

Be grateful
Be present
Be happy

Do more of what makes you happy.

August 14

The planet does not need more successful people. The planet desperately needs more peacemakers, healers, restorers, storytellers, and lovers of all kind.
– Dalai Lama

This is how to be successful:

Be a peacemaker.
Smile.
Be kind.
Extend a hand.
Love.

Be a healer.
Forgive.
Tread gently.
Listen intently.
Love.

Be a restorer.
Give.
See the good.
Express gratitude.
Love.

Be a storyteller.
Live out loud.
Speak the truth.
Honor your word.
Love.
Be a lover.

Of life.
Of yourself.
Of humanity.
Love.

This is all I strive to be.

August 15

Self-talk reflects your innermost feelings.
—Asa Don Brown

Dear Me,

It's been so long since we've talked. And I have so much to say to you. Hard to know where to begin.

Perhaps "I'm sorry" would be the words you most need to hear.

Seems I so often and easily offer forgiveness to others for offenses minor and grand. Yet I rarely extend it your way.

Perhaps "I believe in you would be the words you most need to hear.

Seems I so often and easily let others know of their strength, gifts, and beauty. Yet I rarely share such thoughts with you.

Perhaps "I love you" would be the words you most need to hear.

Seems I so often and easily share the abundance of my love with all who seek me out. Yet I rarely dip you in that well.

And as I end this day, I come to realize so much of the wanting in my life goes away when I forgive, believe in, and love me.

August 16

*We may get knocked down on the outside, but the key to living
in victory is to learn how to get up on the inside.*
—Joel Osteen

There exists something in you
Much greater than any force
Perhaps you forgot it's true
And you have fallen off course

There exists something inside
Much larger than your storm
Perhaps you just let it slide
Allowed excuses to form

There exists something deep
A space where dreams grow
Where promises you keep
A place only you know

You must find that fire
Let nothing cool the heat
When stuck in the mire
You must not choose to retreat

Many names it does go by
Motivation, strength, grit
Courage, heart, will to try
You must never choose to quit

So if the doubt comes calling
You wonder where to begin
To stop the free falling
Simply look deep within.

August 17

You can't do anything for a person who is stuck between being
happy and being miserable. All you can do is get trapped in the
middle, and anyone in the middle just gets squished.
—Jack Gantos

Life is a series of reaching middles. Middle age. Middle of the road. Middle class. Middle ground. Middle of nowhere. If we are not careful, we tend to get stuck in the middle. We sometimes take comfort there. The middle becomes "good enough."

You are not designed for the middle. For settling. You are meant for so much more. Each day you must strive to move forward. No matter the pace, no matter the distance, you need to find a way to just keep moving.

The middle may feel nice. Safe. Comfortable. But here is what I know about comfort: it often leads to complacency. What comes after is often a tendency to fall into old habits.

From there, excuses follow. Without warning, we begin to stumble over small obstacles. The middle is littered with them. Soon they become big hurdles.

When I find myself stuck in the middle, I take a moment to do some soul searching. I remember why I started this journey. I remember what my hopes and dreams are. I remember where I want to go.

Nowhere did the journey ever end with me reaching the middle. So if you are feeling stuck, perhaps it is time to find new inspiration, find a new challenge, recommit to your goals, change things up.

Do not quit in the middle. You don't belong there. Something amazing waits beyond the middle. It might feel scary. That's OK. Most likely it is simply the middle trying to convince you to stay put. It might feel overwhelming. That's OK. Most likely it is simply the middle trying to convince you not to go.

You can do this. You did not come this far to stop in the middle.

August 18

You are the sky. Everything else is just the weather.
—Pema Chodron

You are the sky
Everything else just weather
You are meant to fly
From burdens untether

You are the sun
Everything else just clouds
You are meant to shine for everyone
Life the darkest of shrouds

You are the stars
Everything else just dust
You are to meant to raise the bars
In your brilliance simply trust

You are the universe
Everything else just space
You are never meant to spin in reverse
Go forward to a new place.

You are limitless, not powerless. You are vast and beyond measure. You are so much more than you ever give yourself credit for. You are a child of the heavens, beautiful, and gifted. You are worthy and deserving of that which your soul yearns for.

Dare not to shrink from the grandeur that is you. Spread your wings. Shine. Twinkle. Expand.

August 19

Pain is a pesky part of being human, I've learned it feels like a stab wound to the heart, something I wish we could all do without in our lives here. Pain is a sudden hurt that can't be escaped. But then I have also learned that because of pain, I can feel the beauty, tenderness, and freedom of healing.
—C. JoyBell C.

When I hurt, I have allowed the past to overtake my today.

When I hurt, I have given my power to another.

When I hurt, I have forgotten how to forgive.

When I hurt, I have accepted something not meant for me.

When I hurt, I have focused on the scars over the healing.

When I hurt, I have decided to stand in place rather than moving forward.

When I hurt, I have taken the role of victim in my own life.

When I hurt, I have only myself to blame.

August 20

*When we least expect it, life sets before us a challenge to
test our courage and willingness to change.*
—Paulo Coelho

Perhaps the challenge today
Is to simply let go
To turn and walk away
From what you think you know

Maybe the challenge at hand
Is to simply face your fears
To finally take a stand
Face them in spite of the tears

Is the challenge for you
To finally and simply believe
To go and to finally do
All you are meant to achieve?

Could the challenge be
To simply open your eyes
And to suddenly see
The truth beyond the lies?

What if the challenge ahead
Involves not looking behind
To look forward instead
To be amazed by what you find?

Whatever the challenge for you,
Face it with courage and grace
For here is what is true:
It shall move you to a better place.

August 21

Until you spread you wings you'll have no idea how far you can fly.
—*Napoleon Bonaparte*

I know what you are feeling
Climbed to a new height
The world below now reeling
A heart filled with fright

Standing so close to the ledge
Trying to overcome fears
Fought to get to this new edge
Now fighting back the tears

New fears have now risen
Afraid now to take the leap
Is this horizon now your prison?
Or promises will you keep?

Now not the time to stand still
So embrace the tremblings
Allow courage your heart to fill
Then dare to spread your wings

The freedom it soon brings
When you simply dare to try
Trust in your beautiful wings
And how high you shall fly.

August 22

Far from what I once was but not yet what I'm going to be.
—Anonymous

The past cast a shadow
A darkness over me
To the light I now go
Toward who I am to be

Yesterday left a nasty scar
Marks etched upon my heart
But I have come so very far
The healing may now start

I look back and no longer see
What I had to leave behind
Now but a distant memory
Forward I go, myself to find

I am not there just yet
But moving and on track
Where I've been, won't forget
Yet never going back

Still dreams to be chased
Still miles left to run
New challenges to be faced
My journey not yet done

And whatever should await
I know I shall be ready
I am the keeper of the gate
And I have always held the key.

August 23

I am not what happened to me, I am what I choose to become.
—Carl Gustav Jung

Sadness once called out my name
It wanted to embrace me
I would not play its game
I choose instead to be happy

Bitterness knocked upon my door
It wanted its very own room
I did not live there anymore
I choose to let sweetness bloom

Despair wanted to follow me
To harness me with a rope
I wrestled until I was free
I choose to walk with hope

Failure appeared at every turn
Hoping to create a mess
What failure failed to learn
I choose to be a success

Hatred was sent my way
With my heart it hoped to dance
I simply turned and walked away
I choose to give love another chance

You are not simply a product of events that happen to you.
You do not have to live that way. You can choose to become what you want.

August 24

*From separation and loss, I have learned a lot. I have become strong
and resilient, as is the case of almost every human being exposed
to life and to the world. We don't even know how strong we are
until we are forced to bring that hidden strength forward.*
—Isabel Allende

Perhaps strong is not measured in pounds lifted but rather as a heart pounds with fear.

Perhaps strong is not measured by victories known but rather by defeats overcome.

Perhaps strong is not measured as clenched fists are raised but rather when a hand is merely extended.

Perhaps strong is not measured during the light of day but rather in the darkest of nights.

Perhaps strong is not measured with words spoken but rather with an unspoken resolve.

Perhaps strong is not measured on the way up but rather during the fall.

Perhaps strong is not measured but rather simply lived.

August 25

You are what you believe yourself to be.
—Paulo Coelho

What you ultimately believe
Is what you shall achieve
What exists in your mind
Is all you shall ever find

What you can imagine
Is what you are likely to begin
What you choose to visualize
Is exactly what you will realize

What you decide to think
Determines if you swim or sink
Look closer, you may see
All you were meant to be

More than you give yourself credit for
Capable of so much more
What you should finally know
You're somebody's superhero

You simply must believe.

August 26

*I believe the most important single thing, beyond
discipline and creativity, is daring to dare.*
—*Maya Angelou*

Dare to dare
Dare to care once more

Dare to dream
Dare to scream, "I will"

Dare to try
Dare to fly higher than before

Dare to leap
Dare to keep promises to self

Dare to achieve
Dare to believe in you

Dare to chance
Dare to dance when everyone is watching

Dare to go
Dare to show your heart again

Dare to rise above
Dare to love yourself

Dare to give
Dare to live life full force.

August 27

The greatest battle is not physical but psychological. The demons telling us to give up when we push ourselves to the limit can never be silenced for good. They must always be answered by the quiet steady dignity that simply refuses to give in.
—Graeme Fife

The loudest voice in our ears
Is difficult not to listen to
The screams of our fears
Telling us all we cannot do

Hard to drown them completely out
But it is something that must be done
You must not begin to doubt
This, a battle that must be won

When the demons begin to talk
And their voices grow so loud
Tell them to take a walk
Remain strong, remain proud

For in you a quiet, steady dignity
Again you must call on it
And the demons will finally see
You are not ever going to quit.

August 28

The fight is won or lost far away from witness—behind the lines, in the gym, and out there on the road, long before I dance under those lights.
—Muhammad Ali

Long before the finish line
The battle shall be fought
To failure many must resign
Short of what they sought

Long before the dance
The fight shall be won
Not by mere happenstance
Only if the work is done

Long before the victory
The challenge appears
A test of your bravery
Stand and face your fears

Ahead of you a difficult run
Now write your own story
One of how you got it done
Be a witness to your glory.

August 29

When a man says "I cannot," he has made a suggestion to himself. He has weakened the power of accomplishing that which otherwise would have been accomplished.
—Muhammad Ali

The doubt that you feel
And the fears in you
Are not at all real
Unless you think it true

The wall standing before you
Is just a hallucination
It only comes into view
When you lose sight of the destination

The pain that you face
Meant to help you grow
It cannot slow your pace
You must continue to go

You really *can* do this
If in yourself you believe
Cannot you must dismiss
So that you *can* achieve.

August 30

When you walk with purpose, you collide with destiny.
—Bertice Berry

Have a purpose in mind
Walk steadily toward it
Your destiny you will find
The knowing helps us not to quit

Something beautiful is waiting for you
Perhaps just around the bend
It will come into your view
As indecision comes to an end

So decide what it is you want
Then constantly seek it out
Dreams no longer a taunt
Gone the wonder and doubt

Fulfill your own destiny
Achieve your every goal
All you are meant to be
In the depths of your soul.

August 31

Those at the top of the mountain didn't fall there.
—Marcus Washling

Each mile a dangerous slope
Ahead always a new peak
These we must face with hope
As another challenge we seek

We continue to climb on
A little higher, a little longer
Knowing if our strength is gone
We are simply getting stronger

Today brings another hill
Life asks, "Are you still in?"
Go we must, and so we will
And another climb we begin

Of the height often afraid
And yet on we shall climb
For courage is often made
Just one step at a time

Keep climbing, my friend.
See you at the top.

September 1

When your desires are strong enough, you will appear
to possess superhuman powers to achieve.
—Napoleon Hill

You may possess no exceptional skill
Yet inside a burning desire
Combined with an indomitable will
Your life simply waits to be set on fire

You may have no special talent
Nothing to separate you from the rest
Except you refuse to relent
And always give your very best

You may just be an ordinary person
Who simply chooses to believe
In your ability to get it done
Your impossible you will achieve

With each and every heartbeat
Strength runs through your veins
You have overcome every defeat
Now only the superhero remains

Inside each of us exists a superhero.
They live somewhere between our desire and our will.
If you are looking for a hero, simply look within.

September 2

Remind me that the most fertile lands were built by the fires of volcanoes.
—Andrea Gibson

Used to fear the heat
Afraid of the burning
Bid a hasty retreat
From a slow fire churning

My broken heart remembers
Being charred by the flame
Standing in the dying embers
Never, ever to be the same

Yet the flames draw me in
They seem to grow ever higher
Once more I slowly begin
To move closer to the fire

A match held in my hand
And I create the spark
The flames once again fanned
I will never walk in the dark

The flames no longer consume
Within me a burning desire
My life to once again resume
And to dance within the fire.

September 3

Judge a man by his questions rather than by his answers.
—Voltaire

My soul did ask, "When will you begin?
Can you simply dare to follow me
To places you've never been?
For there, I shall set you free."

My heartbeat said, "Try just once more?"
How will you answer the question?
Shall you take to the dance floor,
Where life and beauty become one?

My spirit pleaded, "Can you move down the road?"
Letting go all the burdens you bear
For in carrying all of yesterday's load
You will rarely arrive anywhere

My life wondered, "Do you dare lasso the sun?"
In my mind was planted a thought
Of life's lessons this a critical one
That which I seek cannot be bought

So many questions inside of me
Yet the answers I already know
For I know where I want to be
And so I choose to simply go.

September 4

Very little is needed to make a happy life; it is all
within yourself, in your way of thinking.
—Marcus Aurelius

You are not a number on a scale or a tag, a waist size, a BMI.
You are much bigger than your body gives you credit for.

You are not a disease, illness, condition, or symptom.
You are becoming healthy, learning to make changes, healing.

You are not your past, a failure, mistakes made.
You are where you are going, still trying, still learning.

You are not weak, broken, empty.
You are strong enough to endure, still standing, full of hope and courage.

You are not the words, opinions, thoughts of others.
You are your daily actions, beliefs held, promises made.

Too often, we define ourselves by a model of deficit,
That which we do not have, what we lack, our perceived flaws.

Today, define yourself from a different mind-set. A different perspective. A model of strength and completeness. A place of self-appreciation and self-love.

Perhaps then you will see you have always been more than you ever imagined.

September 5

*Feeling [unsure] and lost is part of your path. Don't avoid it. See
what those feelings are showing you and use it. Take a breath.
You'll be okay. Even if you don't feel okay all the time.*
—Louis C. K.

The cracks.
In my faith.
Along my path.
On my heart.

They do not mean I am broken. But simply in repair.

The weary.
In my eyes.
Etched on my brow.
In my heart.

It does not mean I am tired of the journey. But simply catching my breath.

The rest.
From the battle.
On this day.
In my heart.

It does not mean I am quitting. But simply gathering strength.

The pain.
Buried deep.
Held quietly.
In my heart.

It does not mean I am suffering. But simply remembering yesterday.

The hope.
That leads me forward.
Kept alive.
In my heart.

It does not mean everything is OK. But simply that it will be.

September 6

...everyone knows that ice cream is worth the trouble of being cold.
Like all things virtuous, you have to suffer to gain the reward.
—Brandon Sanderson

This, another life chat.

Life: I will bend you.
Me: I will not break.

Life: I will make you sore.
Me: I will not submit to the pain.

Life: I will cause you to be winded.
Me: I will not let fear steal my breath.

Life: I will bring burdens to drive you down.
Me: I will not remain there for long.

Life: I will push you to the ledge.
Me: I will use my wings.

Life: I will ask everything of you.
Me: I will give you all I have.

Life: For all of this, I will reward you.
Me: For all of this, I will be grateful.

September 7

I don't like, and even resist, being broken wide-open. But, when the contents of my unconscious self spill out of me and i sift through all the disowned parts of who i am...it's an uncomfortably enlightening and eye-opening experience. It feels a bit like emotional bloodletting. I guess every now and then, i need that release valve to open all the way...
—Jaeda DeWalt

It may be time for a check-up.

1. What you seek awaits just beyond the excuses you accept. If you're still looking, check your excuses.

2. When you need strength, you typically have just enough. If you still doubt, check your history.

3. Where you end up is determined by what you believe you deserve. If you don't like where you are, check your worth.

4. Whatever attitude you bring to a situation shades how you ultimately view the outcome. If you want different results, check your attitude.

5. How you view failing impacts the risks and chances you are willing to take. If you desire more, check your lens.

6. Why you have doubts is in part due to a lack of trust in yourself. If you want to calm the nerves, check your faith.

September 8

It's hard to beat a person who never gives up.
—Babe Ruth

If you must give up, may you give up feeling guilty about taking care of you, being afraid of failing, regretting yesterday, thinking you are unworthy of love.

If you must give up, may you give up making excuses, accepting less than you deserve, looking backward, holding on to what no longer serves you, standing still.

If you must give up, may you give up the ghosts, the demons, the lies that do not define you, the chains that bind you, the notion that you are not good enough.

But you must never give up on a dream. Never give up believing. Never give up on your truth. Never give up trying. Never give up hope. Never give up on love. And never, ever give up on you.

September 9

Replace fear of the unknown with curiosity.
—Penelope Ward

Remember when you were simply free
A life lived out of curiosity
Never fearing to go the distance
It was at your soul's insistence
Remember dancing in the rain
It washed clean any stain
Never fearing the thunder
When once you lived a life of wonder
Remember the playground swings
You soared so high your heart grew wings
Never fearing the fall
You lived to experience it all
Remember the darkness you would explore
Always wanting to know more
Never fearing in the dark what might be
You shined your light for all to see.

Something has happened along the way
Curiosity gone, fear runs the day
No longer singing in the rain
You've chosen to fear the pain
Where once you soared so high
Now afraid to touch the sky
Despite the clouds all around
You've chosen to remain on the ground
The darkness now holds a fear

The demons seem so very near
Despite your brilliant light
You've chosen to keep it hidden from sight
My challenge for you this day
Find the curious that went away
See the wonder, choose to fly
Shine your light, give it a try.

We do not know what the day has in store
Have the curiosity to explore
Fear no longer a powerful thing
Return to living instead of existing.

September 10

The reason birds can fly and we can't is simply because they
have perfect faith, for to have faith is to have wings.
—J. M. Barrie

I am at a point in life where it would seem I should know my answers by now.

For I've learned. I've grown. I've lived.

And yet it seems there is still much for me to find out. So many questions sit unanswered.

Wheres and whens and whys.

Where am I heading? When shall I arrive? Why is the journey leading me to this place?

So many questions sit unanswered. And yet the unknown does not bring fear or doubt.

I have faith that where I am headed is where my life's compass was always meant to point. My life's true north. And I simply trust.

I have faith I will arrive when I am meant to get there. My life's true pace. And I can be patient.

I have faith the journey is leading me to this place because it is following my heart. My life's true purpose. And this I know is love.

I have faith. For I've learned. I've grown. I've lived.

September 11

As soon as you trust yourself, you will know how to live.
—Johann Wolfgang von Goethe

Life asks some difficult questions. This. Another life chat.

Life: Why do you stand at the edge?
Me: I am wondering if I should take the leap.

Life: Why don't you just jump?
Me: I am afraid.

Life: What do you fear most?
Me: The falling.

Life: What is the worst that could happen?
Me: I get hurt again.

Life: What if I told you I will catch you?
Me: I still have fear.

Life: You do not trust me?
Me: I do not trust myself.

Life: Want to know the truth?
Me: Always.

Life: When you learn to trust yourself, nevermore shall you fear.
Me: ...(sigh)...

September 12

When my eyes meet his gaze as we're sitting here staring at each other, time stops. Those eyes are piercing mine, and I can swear at this moment he senses the real me. The one without the attitude, without the façade.
—Simone Elkeles

Sometimes I cannot help but stare.

Pardon my stare. Think me not rude or impolite. For it is not your blemishes or imperfections from which I cannot avert my gaze. I am simply in awe of your incomparable beauty.

Pardon my stare. Think me not afraid or filled with doubt. For it is not your darkness or storms from which I cannot avert my gaze. I am simply taken by the wonder of your light.

Pardon my stare. Think me not confused or mistrusting. For it is not your secrets or unknowns from which I cannot avert my gaze. I am simply captured by the mystery of you.

Pardon my stare. Think me not far- or near-sighted. Nor is it through rose-colored glasses from which I view you. I have simply fallen in love with all I see in you.

I wonder: when you stare out at your life, what do you see?

September 13

In case you never get a second chance: don't be afraid! And
what if you do get a second chance? You take it!
—C. JoyBell C.

You've been given another chance.

To forgive

To improve

To make mistakes

To dream big

To laugh and smile

To make amends

To spread your wings

To start again

To choose joy

To breathe deeply

To give freely

To dance

To change course

To fall in love.

You've been given another chance.

It's called today. It is waiting for you.

September 14

*I was smiling yesterday, I am smiling today and I will smile
tomorrow. Simply because life is too short to cry for anything.*
—Santosh Kalwar

There is always a reason to smile.

The sun came up

It found you breathing

You have another chance

Today is all yours

The road awaits

The possibilities are endless

You are in control

Hope exists

You have all you need

There is no fear

You made it here

Life is good

You are loved

There is always a reason to smile.

Always.

September 15

It's what you choose to believe that makes you the person you are.
—Karen Marie Moning

I believe in...

Morning snuggles
Love removes the struggles
A kitchen dance party
Love is never tardy
Playing in the rain
Love eases every pain
The morning cup of coffee
Love sets you free
Hiking unknown trails
Love is in the details
Sipping cold lemonade
Love is not manmade
Singing your favorite song
Love is never wrong
A pajama sort of day
Love always finds a way
Enjoying the little things
Love is a set of wings
Happy ever after
Love is life's laughter
Sunday-morning drives
Love suddenly arrives
A walk among the pines
Love exists between the lines.

September 16

*Through the many years of what I thought was "searching"
was really the process of "awakening."*
—Ka Chinery

I woke up in love this morning. In love with this place I am in. Right here. Right now. Where I am. As I am.

I woke up in love this morning. In love with the unknown of today. The mystery of what awaits. The wonder of newness.

I woke up in love this morning. In love with the dream. That which I dream with eyes open. That which is coming true.

I woke up in love this morning. In love with the song my life is playing. Lyrics still learning. Yet a melody my heart has always known.

I woke up in love this morning. In love with this one precious, beautiful life. It fulfills everything I need. Holds everything I want.

I woke up in love this morning. In love with all of this. All because I woke up simply loving myself.

September 17

...I ask you right here please to agree with me that a scar is never ugly. That is what the scar makers want us to think. But you and I, we must make an agreement to defy them. We must see all scars as beauty. Okay? This will be our secret. Because take it from me, a scar does not form on the dying. A scar means, I survived.
—Chris Cleave

These scars. Ones seen. These scars. Ones not visible. I have earned. For I wrested my demons. Did battle with my fears. In search of peace. For I am worthy.

These bruises. Deep and aching. These bruises. Fading and yellowed. I have earned. For I stumbled along the way. Fell so many times. In search of dreams. For I am worthy.

These fine lines. Etched upon my brow. These fine lines. Tracing my trials. I have earned. For I squinted at the brilliance of my own light. Peered deep into my darkness. In search of truth. For I am worthy.

These burn marks. Upon my flesh. These burn marks. In my heart. I have earned. For I dared dance in the flames. Opened my heart to the fire. In search of love. For I am worthy.

This life. The pain. This life. The beauty. I have earned. For I grew to understand my worth.

September 18

Gratitude is not only the greatest of virtues, but the parent of all others.
—Marcus Tullius Cicero

This, my love letter to my life.

Dear Life,

I am so filled with gratitude for you. For all the lessons you have taught me. The small, the grand, the difficult. Even if I did not always understand what you were trying to teach me. You allowed me to learn and become.

I am so filled with gratitude for you. For all the patience you have shown me. The times I was wrong, weak, broken. You never gave up on me. You allowed me to grow at my own pace.

I am trying to honor you. Less complaining. More acceptance. Less whining. More understanding. Fewer times shall I try to have you conform to my expectations of how this is supposed to go. More time allowing you to simply unfold as you are meant to.

I am trying to honor you. Trusting. Letting go. Looking forward. Believing in the path you have laid before me. No matter how long it takes for me to arrive.

I am so filled with love for you. So captured by your light, beauty, and magic. A light so rare. A beauty unparalleled. A magic unexplained. I need not look very far or deep, for it is simply how you arrive. I must only choose to see it.

I am so filled with love for you. The grandeur, the mystery, the wonder of you. I stand in awe of your grandeur. So much you have to offer me. Captivated by your mystery. So much I long to know. It is the very wonder of you that takes my breath away.

All my love, Me

September 19

Sometimes your joy is the source of your smile, but sometimes your smile can be the source of your joy.
—Thich Nhat Hanh

Life and I spent a little time chatting today.

Life: What do you have to smile about?
Me: I have everything to smile about.

Life: But I have stripped away so much from you. There should be tears for all you have lost.
Me: I am smiling for remembering all I have ever been given.

Life: But I have broken so many paths of yours. There should be tears for all the dead ends.
Me: I am smiling for learning the road I am truly meant to walk.

Life: But I have inflicted so much pain upon you. There should be tears for all the hurt you know.
Me: I am smiling for knowing I am healing.

Life: But I have shattered so many dreams of yours. There should be tears for all the broken dreams.
Me: I am smiling for always having the chance to dream again.

Life: But I don't understand. After all I've done to you, how could you still be smiling?
Me: Life, you should know. For you taught me to smile.

September 20

However mean your life is, meet it and live it; do not shun it and call it hard names. It is not so bad as you are. It looks poorest when you are richest. The fault-finder will find faults even in paradise. Love your life, poor as it is. You may perhaps have some pleasant, thrilling, glorious hours, even in a poorhouse.
—Henry David Thoreau

It will simply hurt.

But from this, you shall become strong.

It will be a test.

But from this, you shall learn.

It will bring doubt.

But from this, you shall find your truth.

It will cause fear.

But from this, you shall come to know courage.

It will not relent.

But from this, you shall persist.

It will be hard.

But from this, you shall not bow.

It will push you down.

But from this, you shall rise.

It is life. And from this, you shall have lived.

September 21

You might be looking for reasons but there are no reasons.
—Nina LaCour

Here's your pep talk.
You don't need a reason.

To do
To run
To laugh
To dare
To explore
To smile
To risk
To dance
To hope
To be grateful
To leap
To shine
To change
To believe
To pray
To give
To fly
To trust
To go
To sing
To love

You don't need a reason.
You are the reason.

You've just been pep talked.

September 22

Love simply is.
—Paulo Coelho

Love does not have an agenda.

It does not write out its script.

It simply unfolds.

Love does not require approval.

It does not yield to opinion.

It simply happens.

Love does not wither under pressure.

It does not wilt in the heat.

It simply endures.

Love does not demand changes.

It does not force itself.

It simply accepts.

Love does not doubt.

It does not question its own truth.

It simply believes.

Love does not wait until the timing is perfect.

It does not arrive on a set schedule.

It simply shows up.

Love. It simply is.

September 23

When you make a choice, you change the future.
—Deepak Chopra

You choose...

Shadows or light
Give up or fight
Courage or fright

Joy or sorrow
Give or borrow
Today or tomorrow

Forgive or forget
Accept or regret
Trust or fret

Humility or pride
Seek or hide
Follow or guide

Smile or frown
Swim or drown
Up or down

Peace or war
Less or more
Stand or soar

Fear or dare
Selfish or share
Stand by or care

Jump or wait
Growth or stagnate
Love or hate

Either or. You always get to choose.

September 24

As love leads the way, the steps will be made easy.
—David Scott

This, a letter to love.

Dear Love,

All my life, I've been running.
Longing. Aching. Searching. Lost.

All my life, I've been running.
From the past. My ghosts. A brokenness.

All my life, I've been running.
Afraid. Alone. Empty. Starving.

All my life, I've been running.
Out of time. Out of doubt. Out of fear.

All my life, I've been running.
Confused. Unsure. Impatient. Struggling.

All my life, I've been running.
Toward the light. Toward the unknown. Toward a peace.

All my life, I've been running.
Hope-filled. Believing. Trusting. Knowing.

All my life, I've been running.
Finally realizing I have always been running to you.

Love, Me

September 25

I'm in love with you, and I'm not in the business of denying myself the simple pleasure of saying true things. I'm in love with you, and I know that love is just a shout into the void, and that oblivion is inevitable, and that we're all doomed and that there will come a day when all our labor has been returned to dust, and I know the sun will swallow the only earth we'll ever have, and I am in love with you.
—John Green

Dear Life,

You ask why I love you.

You bring out the best in me.

You make me want to be better.

You challenge, push, break me.

You are my salvation, my peace.

You take me to the edge.

You accept me where I am.

You cure the ache.

You are freedom.

You quicken my pulse.

You leave me breathless.

You change me.

You take me places I've never been before.

You are now a part of me.

You ask why I love you. Now you know.

Love, Me

September 26

Instead of saying, "I'm damaged, I'm broken, I have trust issues"
say, "I'm healing, I'm rediscovering myself, I'm starting over."
—Horacio Jones

This, a story.

The edges a bit chipped. Perhaps some say pieces are broken.

The surface a bit scratched. Perhaps some say scarred.

The colors a bit faded. Perhaps some say dulled too much.

The age a bit showing. Perhaps some say simply too worn.

And so this piece gets stamped "damaged goods." And a discount sticker placed for all to see.

Until someone comes along. And smooths out the edges. With a gentle touch.

Until someone comes along. And understands the scars are merely beauty marks.

Until someone comes along. And shines a new light, restoring the brilliance.

Until someone comes along. And something brand new is created.

And so this piece is fully restored. And a "priceless" sticker placed for all to see.

Moral of the story: There are no damaged goods. Merely pieces waiting for someone to come along.

September 27

*At the end of the day the only questions I will ask myself are...Did
I love enough? Did I laugh enough? Did I make a difference?*
—Katrina Mayer

I could not possibly love enough.
For my love is limitless.
I shall try to empty myself.

I could not possibly love enough.
For my love is ever growing.
I shall try to not contain it.

I could not possibly love enough.
For my love is meant for another.
I shall try to give it all away.

I could not possibly laugh enough.
For laughter is my soul's breath.
I shall try to simply exhale.

I could not possibly laugh enough.
For laughter is a master key.
I shall try to open every door.

I could not possibly laugh enough.
For laughter is an unending song.
I shall try to sing from the heart.

And, thus, I shall hope to have made a difference.

September 28

Something amazing happens when we surrender and just love. We melt
into another world, a realm of power already within us. The world
changes when we change. The world softens when we soften.
The world loves us when we choose to love the world.
—Marianne Williamson

Today, I will surrender.
Laying down the weapons I have used against myself.
Harsh tones, worn excuses, self-pity.
I will give in to love.

Today, I will surrender.
No more fighting against what I am worthy of.
My hopes, desires, dreams.
I will give in to love.

Today, I will surrender.
Putting down the weights that do not strengthen me.
Worry, regret, fear.
I will give in to love.

Today, I will surrender.
Refusing to believe what is no longer true.
Yesterday, failure, weakness.
I will give in to love.

Today, I will surrender.
Doubting less that which I am sure of.
Light, faith, love.
I will give in to love.

Today, I surrender. I give in to love.

September 29

It is difficult to soar to your destiny carrying the burden of doubt,
impossible to soar to your destiny carrying the burden of fear, but
conceivable to soar to your destiny carried by the wings of faith.
—Matshona Dhliwayo

We all have a "something."

What is that something you cannot stop thinking about?
That you once never even imagined?

What is that something you already miss?
That you have never even had?

What is that something you ache for?
That you have never even felt?

What is that something you reach for?
That you have never even touched?

What is that something you daydream about?
That you have never even seen?

What is that something that calls your name?
That you have never even spoken to?

What is that something? It is your destiny.
And you must go to it. It is waiting patiently for you to arrive.

September 30

This thing about you that you think is your flaw—
it's the reason I'm falling in love with you.
—Colleen Hoover

I have fallen in love.
With the possibilities.
My fears.
This moment.

I have fallen in love.
With the unknown.
My hopes.
This dream.

I have fallen in love.
With the power of choice.
My worth.
This day.

I have fallen in love.
With the wonder.
My path.
This space.

I have fallen in love.
With the always.
My destiny.
This beautiful life.

I have fallen in love.
All over again.

October 1

Talking about our problems is our greatest addiction.
Break the habit. Talk about your joys.
—Rita Schiano

You want to speak of weakness when you are strong in so many ways. To keep rising after being knocked down. Strength. To keep fighting when defeat seems imminent. Strength.

You want to speak of emptiness when your life is filled with so many blessings. A brand-new day. Blessing. A beating heart. Blessing.

You want to speak of failure when you have succeeded at so much. You made it through to the light again today. Success. You have not given up. Success.

You want to speak of fear when you are so very brave. You are facing the unknowns. Courage. You are trembling but are willing to leap. Courage.

You want to speak of hopelessness when you have so much to believe in. Your strength. Your blessings. Your successes. Your courage.

Before you speak, listen. And in the pause between hearing and saying, you will know the truth of your life. Speak that.

October 2

Teach all men to fish, but first teach all men to be fair. Take less, give more.
Give more of yourself, take less from the world. Nobody
owes you anything, you owe the world everything.
—Suzy Kassem

If given but one more breath, I would give it to you.
So you may simply exhale.

If given but one more wish, I would give it to you.
So you may simply know someone wishes you joy.

If given but one more heartbeat, I would give it to you.
So you may simply feel an unconditional love.

If given but one more smile, I would give it to you.
So you may simply see how beautiful it looks on you.

If given but one more moment, I would give it to you.
So you may simply experience the gift of unhurried time.

If given but one more sunrise, I would give it to you.
So you may simply understand the endless possibilities before you.

And if given all this, may you simply know a beautiful day.

October 3

Love is the sister to Truth, but they differ in two ways. You must go to Truth to find her. She will never come looking for you. However, you are never to go looking for her sister Love. Love will find you in your own divine timing, when you are ready for her. So don't look, she will come. She always does.
—Suzy Kassem

This, another life chat.

Me: Where do I find love?
Life: You don't. Love finds you.

Me: When will it find me?
Life: Love arrives when you need it most.

Me: How will it know?
Life: Love listens. It will hear your heart. So always speak its language.

Me: What if I'm not ready?
Life: Love has its own calendar.

Me: Do we have space for love?
Life: There is ample room. Love fills all the empty spaces.

Me: What will love do for us?
Life: Love. It will do all the things love does.

Me: Do you know of these things?
Life: Comfort. Serenity. Warmth. Hope. Always. Love does this.

Me: How will I know it's love?

Life: Love has a feeling all its own. You will know.

Me: What does it feel like?

Life: Love. It feels like coming home.

October 4

Fear is just as real as belief. Choose wisely.
—Unknown

Do you ever stop to think of the tremendous power you possess?

All contained in the simple ability to choose.

Consider this. You can choose your path, attitude, response, thoughts, outlook, disposition, truth, words, actions, beliefs, and dreams.

I have been told that I am not keeping it real for viewing the world and this life through such a positive lens.

The truth is that I have simply learned of the limitless power I have to impact my own life and how I now choose to live it.

Where fear once resided, belief now exists. By choice.

Where pain once lived, joy has moved in. By choice.

Where doubt eroded away the walls, trust has built a new foundation. By choice.

Where suffering held me captive, love has set me free. By choice.

I may have it wrong. But I choose to believe otherwise.

And I have made the choice to live life full force.

October 5

Once you become consciously aware of just how powerful your thoughts are,
you will realize everything in your life is exactly how you allow it to be.
—Melanie Moushigian Koulouris

Where my thoughts go
Is where I am led
Reaping what I sow
For the voice in my head

Where thoughts take me
I am bound to follow
Ultimately this, my destiny
Chained to what I know

Where my thoughts fall
I focus all my energy
When they become small
Only then do I fail me

Thoughts allow negative in
Trapping me where I've been
It is time for them to begin
Allowing me to be free again.

October 6

Hold fast to dreams, for if dreams die
Life is a broken-winged bird that cannot fly.
—Langston Hughes

Become your very own dream
It is something we all can do
Not as far-fetched as it may seem
This is a dream that can come true

Let it begin with the way you talk
Watch your words, for you hear it all
How you carry yourself when you walk
Keep your chin up, be brave, stand tall

Shine your light for others to see
Believe in the magic that is purely you
Trust yourself and your own journey
Do not be afraid to begin anew

Stop residing with doubt and fear
Quiet those voices from your head
It's OK to lead your own cheer
Start living with faith instead

Imagine being the one you dream of
If you could see in you what others see
It begins from a place of true self-love
And from there you can simply be.

Be your dream.

October 7

Today is a victory over yourself of yesterday.
—Miyamoto Musashi

Dear Yesterday,

No longer interested in your game
Not willing to play it again
I will not feel any more shame
For where my life has been

You want to whisper in my ear
Reminders of what used to be
But I no longer despise or fear
Your old and faded picture of me

My dreams you wait to attack
So razor-sharp is your knife
On you, I've turned my back
You're no longer welcome in my life

It is time for you to go away
And simply fade from view
Got no time for you today
I've got better things to do

You are but a fading memory
What you cannot comprehend
From your chains I am free
And I am finally on the mend.

October 8

Sometimes our walls exist just to see who has the strength to knock them down.
—Darnell Lamont Walker

No matter the direction I go
The wall will still be there
Pain I will once again know
I've suffered more than my share

Every time I've faced the wall
Seems it did all the hitting
Forced me to crawl
Made me feel like quitting

Every time I've faced the wall
I am unable to contend
Once again I take the fall
Dreams come to an end

Every time I've faced the wall
It has grown to mythical size
In its shadow I appear small
My fear I cannot disguise

Yet each time I face the wall
I come to grow ever stronger
It may again test my all
But I shall fear it no longer

Yet each time I face the wall
I grow steadier in my resolve
My pace it cannot stall
My faith shall not dissolve

I will face the wall again today
I won't be knocked off track
If it dares to stand in my way
I plan on hitting back.

October 9

To conquer frustration, one must remain intensely
focused on the outcome, not the obstacles.
—T. F. Hodge

What you face is not easy. Never discount it.

Do not forget to treat yourself with grace.

What sits before you may feel impossible. It just may be.

Do not feel like a failure.

What hurts you is real. It might have broken another.

Do not forget your strength.

What path you walk is a challenge. By definition it will test you.

Do not focus on the obstacles.

What the day holds is always unknown. And you may not be prepared.

Do not let that frighten you.

What you must remember most is that you have always found a way through.
Always.

This will be no different.

October 10

We make a living by what we get. We make a life by what we give.
—Winston Churchill

May I give away all my gratitude
Expressing thanks for those in my day.

May I give away all my prayers
Silently speaking for those in need.

May I give away all my light
Shining it for those still searching.

May I give away all my kindness
Offering it for those seeking a hand.

May I give away all my love
Filling the spaces for those around me.

May I give away all I have
For this I have come to know:

My vessel can only be filled if I am willing to empty it completely.

October 11

*Perfectionism is not a quest for the best. It is a pursuit of the worst in ourselves,
the part that tells us that nothing we do will ever be good enough.*
—Julia Cameron

In our pursuit of perfection
So much we have is lost
We lose our true direction
Our gifts ignored and tossed

You need not seek to be perfect
We exist as a beautiful mess
Our flaws are not a defect
Embrace your own humanness

Perfection is so overrated
And demands such a toll
Pieces of ourselves hated
Leaving wounds upon the soul

Upon much closer inspection
Every line, curve, and scar
Each perfect imperfection
Is the beauty of who you are.

October 12

Age wrinkles the body. Quitting wrinkles the soul.
—Douglas MacArthur

I could not see it then
Quitting exacts a toll
Could have stayed where I've been
Going on saved my very soul

Quitting leaves an indelible mark
In the depths of one's heart
Pushing through creates a spark
A raging fire about to start

Comes the tired, comes the pain
You must look beyond it
You must remember this refrain:
"I simply refuse to quit"

It will require courage and desire
Not always easy to push through
Quitting it is the ultimate liar
Never speaking what you can do

When I thought no more could I give
Decided not to give in to it
It's when I truly started to live
For choosing not to quit.

October 13

For broken dreams the cure is, dream again. Dream deeper.
—C. S. Lewis

My Dear Friend,

Do not be fooled into thinking there is but one dream for you. For dreams are as the stars. They light our darkest nights, brighten our path, and appear in abundance to guide us. So many to choose from.

Do not fear to dream again. For dreams are as the seasons. They change over time and as each new one arrives, we find reason to celebrate. So much to rejoice in.

Do not mourn too long the end of a dream once held. For dreams are as grains of sands. We may hold them for a time, but slowly many slip through our hands. A precious few will stay with us. Make your peace and then let some slip away.

Dream, my friend. Dream again. Dream deeper.

October 14

A broken heart is just the growing pains necessary so that you can love more completely when the real thing comes along.
—J. S. B. Morse

I have not walked in your shoes
I know not of your strength
This road you did not choose
So unsure of its length

I have not felt your sadness
I know not the tears you shed
This road filled with madness
So unsure of what lies ahead

I have not lived your ache
I know not how it must feel
Praying that day will break
The nightmares are all too real

Yet I know of your heart
The joy contained within
To open the cage is a start
Soon the healing can begin

Yet I know of your history
Courage I see in your eyes
A brighter day you will see
And again you shall rise

Yet I know of your spirit
It is once more calling out
Listen and you will hear it
Hope triumphs doubt

Yet I know of your love
Its healing capacity
As unending as heaven above
The love will always be.

October 15

When I was five years old, my mother always told me the key to life was
happiness. When I went to school, they asked me what I wanted to be
when I grew up. I wrote down "happy." They told me I didn't understand
the assignment, and I told them they didn't understand life.
—John Lennon

We tend to complicate things. Often questioning what we already know in our hearts. Believing the answers cannot be so simple. Thus, giving in to our inner cynic. Forgetting the childlike wonder through which we once viewed this life. And forever losing the key we once held.

It really is simple. The key to life is found in all the little joys we take for granted, we no longer allow ourselves, we now overlook. The key to life is contained within all the fleeting moments when we remember and smile, when we give ourselves permission to slow down, when we allow gratitude to fill us up.

Call me an optimist if you must. I simply still believe in the magic, wonder, and beauty of this life. I simply still believe in miracles, happy endings, the power of faith, and love.

And, thus, I hold the key to my own life. And I choose to use it to unlock my own happiness.

October 16

Life always begins with one step outside of your comfort zone.
—Shannon L. Alder

I came to the end of my trail
Where a path no more existed
Felt vulnerable and frail
"Keep walking," faith insisted

I walked to the end of my world
Ahead many scary things
Into the abyss myself I hurled
And simply trusted my wings

I went to the edge of my universe
Beyond all I'd ever known
A chance to hear a new verse
Just past my comfort zone

I arrived at my self-imposed limit
Had placed these chains on me
Here I am not meant to quit
If I am ever to be free

Do not fear the unknown.
Fear never having explored what lies beyond your limits.

410

October 17

Nobody can hurt me without my permission.
—Mahatma Gandhi

Last night, I walked into the desert under the brilliance and baeauty of a full moon. There in the silence, my life spoke clearly to me.

This is what I heard: "Without your permission, you cannot be held down, held back, held under."

So I slowly stretched my arms wide open for the universe to see. And I wrote down these words:

The authors of lies
Hoped to bury the truth
They did not succeed
For I am writing my story

The bringers of darkness
Tried to cast out the light
They were unable
For I refused to be dimmed

The keepers of dreams
Wanted to put them out of reach
They could not
For I would not stop climbing

The makers of chains
Sought to imprison my spirit
They simply failed
For I live with arms wide open.

October 18

When we love, we always strive to become better than we are. When we strive to become better than we are, everything around us becomes better too.
—Paulo Coelho

When love arrives, what shall I have to offer it?

My attention.
For this is how love is nourished.

My understanding.
For this is how love learns.

My truth.
For this is how love finds comfort.

My patience.
For this is how love unfolds.

My affection.
For this is how love shines.

My kindness.
For this is how love works.

My unselfishness.
For this is how love gives.

My time.
For this is how love grows.

My love.
For this is how love stays.

My everything.
For this is what love offers me.

October 19

A man who dares to waste one hour of time has not discovered the value of life.
—Charles Darwin

If time were all I had, I would waste not another second on worry or fear.

If time were all I had, I would be more aware of how I spend this valuable currency.

If time were all I had, I would invest more of it in all that which I love.

If time were all I had, I would fill it with joy, laughter, and love.

If time were all I had, I would slow my breathing and my pace.

If time were all I had, I would live every moment as if it were my last.

Knowing time is all I have, I have changed how I will live the time given me.

October 20

Lift your eyes, straighten your back, let fear and pain
walk away like the turtles they are.
—Victor Robert Lee

On the other side Your freedom waits
From fear you mustn't hide
Let it in, open its gates.

Face fear head on
Look deep into its eyes
Soon it will be gone
For it was always a disguise.

You simply need shine a light
And your fears will run
The time is now right
To do what must be done.

If fear keeps you chained
You just don't see
It cannot keep you contained
Your courage is the key.

A life filled with fear
Becomes one of regret
I hope this you hear
You are larger than any fear you've ever met.

So go ahead and dream
Dream dreams so grand
Fears are not what they seem
This you must understand.

The very paradox of fear
It invites you to become
When its whisper you hear
Ahead awaits your freedom.

October 21

It's a funny thing coming home. Nothing changes. Everything looks the same,
feels the same, even smells the same. You realize what's changed is you.
—*F. Scott Fitzgerald*

I've taken the long way home
An endless journey for peace
Alone, I was forced to roam
Until the voices cease.

They whispered every day
Their echoes reverberated
"Not good enough," they say
Parts of me I once hated.

And so my journey went on
As I searched high and low
For where my faith had gone
For the me I once did know.

I looked in the familiar places
All of my yesterdays
I looked in the familiar spaces
All my old ways.

I could not find me there
For there I refused to reside
I could not find me anywhere
Until I looked deep inside.

And what I did learn
I am beautifully me
The voices no longer burn
Time to come home, I am finally free.

October 22

Just because I laugh a lot doesn't mean my life is easy. Just because I have a smile on my face every day doesn't mean that something is not bothering me. I just choose to move on, and not dwell on all the negatives in my life. Every new moment gives me the chance to renew anew. I choose to be that.
—Unknown

Given just so many grains of sand.
They are precious and few
As they slip through your hand
With them, what will you do?

For time passes too quickly
To spend much being mad
Perhaps you forget to see
All the blessings you had.

All you can ever save
From moments that passed
Memories of what you gave
What thoughts will you let last?

As for me, I know my choice
I shall find my own peace
Use a more gentle voice
I shall let the worry cease.

As for me, I know my course
I shall find my own light
And shine it full force
To brighten the darkest night.

I shall choose this just because
At the very end of the day
It is simply who I was
And I knew no other way.

October 23

Do what you can, with what you have, where you are.
—Theodore Roosevelt

It's about today.
Right here.
Right now.
Not the past.
That story was written.
Reading it over and over will not change the ending.
Not tomorrow.
That is an unwritten check.
And you cannot cash it.

It's about today and what you will choose to do with it.
Excuses or results.
Stay stuck or move forward.
The choice has always been yours.

It's not about you can't do.
You've worked from that file long enough to have it memorized, validated, and approved.
Time to delete that outdated, worn, and corrupted file.

It's about what you can do.
You are an amazing, talented, and gifted being.
When did you stop giving yourself permission to believe in you?
Knock it off. You are far more capable than you have ever given yourself credit for.
Go get it done.

It's not about where you want to be.

It's not about five pounds lighter.

Two minutes faster.

A higher pay grade.

Bigger house.

Those don't make you who you are.

Let me repeat: those do not make you who you are.

It's about where you are right now.

You are good enough.

You are worthy.

How about you begin talking to yourself and treating yourself in that fashion?

You deserve that.

Right here and now.

October 24

Very often it's the last key on the key ring that opens the lock. Don't you dare give up.
—Rev. Run

You have always held the keys.

To every lock.

To every closed door.

To the cell you built.

It is time to use those keys.

Heart: You can do this.

Trust: The lock will turn.

Strength: Push the door open.

Courage: Face what's behind the door.

Hope: Something better awaits.

Faith: You will get there.

October 25

Live your life without ever having to ask, "What if?"
—Ken Poirot

I still have my fears, my doubts, my questions.

They live in the recesses of my mind. Buried. Seemingly dormant. And yet I know they are there. For in the quiet, they awaken, and they whisper to me.

My fears whisper in tones of "what if?" "What if you fail? What if you fall? What if you get hurt again?" And they want to keep me from trying.

My doubts whisper in tones of "you cannot." "You cannot do this. You cannot get up again. You cannot continue to believe." And they want to keep me from trusting myself.

My questions whisper in tones of "who are you?" "Who are you to dream so big? Who are you to think you are worthy of this? Who are you to shine your light?" And they want to keep me from the life I deserve.

I still have my fears, my doubts, my questions. In the quiet, they awaken, and they whisper to me.

And without a word, I simply jump. And the whispers are no more.

October 26

The problem, often not discovered until late in life, is that when you look for things in life like love, meaning, motivation, it implies they are sitting behind a tree or under a rock. The most successful people in life recognize, that in life they create their own love, they manufacture their own meaning, they generate their own motivation.
—*Neil deGrasse Tyson*

This really isn't about motivation, mojo, or if you're feeling it.

This really isn't a should, could, would, or need to.

This really isn't for your ex, your current, your next, or anyone else.

This really isn't about Monday or any other day on the calendar.

This really isn't about a race or a goal or a challenge.

This is simply about you, in this moment, doing what serves your good.

This is simply about you understanding your worth and treating yourself like you are worthy.

This is simply about you believing in your strength, coming to realize the power you possess.

This is simply about you taking control of your situation and making the changes you desire.

This is simply about you. And when you come to recognize that as the simple truth, everything else will fall into place.

You've just been pep talked.

October 27

Striving for successful goals will have a tendency at times to be discouraging, thankless, and mentally draining. You are entitled to these feelings, however you are not entitled to give up.
—DeWayne Owens

Quitting comes so easily
A simple letting go
Happens so gradually
So you hardly even know

The once-brilliant fire slowly dies
As we give in to the quit
Despite a few half-hearted tries
To keep the flame lit

Darkness then fills the space
Comes the shadows of doubt
But we settle for this place
Stop seeking a way out

Yet too much is at stake
You have come so very far
But more steps still to take
Do not stop where you are

You are bigger than the quit
It is no measure for your heart
It cannot contain your spirit
Again today, dare to start

You are too strong to give in
Even if weakness should arrive
This battle you must win
You must keep the flame alive

There is something you must know
You have always been worth it
Time to now get up and go
Do not allow yourself to quit.

October 28

Unless it is mad, passionate, extraordinary love, it is a waste of time. There are too many mediocre things in life. Love should not be one of them.
—Unknown

Fall completely in love with you
An affair passionate and true
Of such a love you are worthy
Love your scars and beauty.

Self-love should simply amaze
It should set your world ablaze
Loving you changes everything
Light and joy it will bring.

When you love yourself so deep
Such love to yourself you cannot keep
It becomes a love that does grow
Spreading to everyone you know.

An extraordinary love is waiting
Your heart is anticipating
For too long kept it on the shelf
The time has come to love yourself.

October 29

*My heart might be bruised, but it will recover and become capable of seeing
beauty of life once more. It's happened before, it will happen again, I'm sure. When
someone leaves, it's because someone else is about to arrive. I'll find love again.*
—Paulo Coelho

You arrived unexpectedly. For either I was not looking for you, or my eyes were closed to you. But when I awoke today, you were there. And I whispered, "Hello, beautiful."

You arrived quietly. For either I was not listening for you, or I simply refused to hear you. But when I awoke today, you were there. And I whispered, "Hello, beautiful."

You arrived suddenly. For either I was not prepared for you, or you showed up without warning. But when I awoke today, you were there. And I whispered, "Hello, beautiful."

You arrived without fanfare. For either I was not paying attention to the signs, or you do not trumpet your arrival. But when I awoke today, you were there. And I whispered, "Hello, beautiful."

You arrived. And when I awoke today, you were there. And I whispered, "Hello, love."

October 30

*Sometimes we truly begin to find ourselves when we are so broken
and weak...and in that moment a spark ignites and we dig down
and find the strength to stand strong and fight on.*
—Kim Bayne

I lost myself among the pieces of a dream shattered.
The shards pierced my will.
Left weakened.
Devoid of hope.
Broken.

Yet I found myself amid the wreckage.
For in the reflection of those pieces, I caught a glimpse.
That of the silhouette of a fighter.
And I recognized it as my own shadow.

And in the dying embers of a smothered dream, a spark took hold.
Until it burned again white-hot.
A new day dawned a new dream.
And I found the strength to fight on.

October 31

*Out of suffering have emerged the strongest souls; the
most massive characters are seared with scars.*
—Kahlil Gibran

I have been seared.
The flames danced upon my soul.
The scars invisible.
For they are worn inside.

Days I still feel the heat.
I am still vulnerable.
Times the wounds lay open.
The pain is exquisite.
Excruciating.

But still I rise.
For I have been forged of hope.
Designed to persevere.
My spirit daily reborn.
My soul renewed.
I am strong. I am a miracle.

November 1

One's destination is never a place, but a new way of seeing things.
—Henry Miller

Once so bent on looking to the past, I could not envision a future.

Once so blinded by the tears, I could not look beyond the pain.

Once so in love with the lies, I could not find my truths.

Once so afraid of moving forward, I lost sight of my path.

Once so believing the world had stopped turning, I could not see the sun rise.

Once so imprisoned by regret, I never knew I held the key to the prison door.

Once. Nevermore. I stopped looking back. The tears no longer fall. I know the truth. My path is clear. The sun came up again today. I pardoned myself.

I arrived where I am supposed to be when I saw things in a new light.
Vision leads you home.

November 2

Love in such a way the person you love feels free.
—Thich Nhat Hanh

If it is love, it offers wings
Not bindings as chains or rope
If it is love, it simply brings
The gift of hope.

If it is love, it fills you up
Not draining or able to empty
If it is love, it overflows your cup
Never to leave you thirsty.

If it is love, It owes nothing
It demands no cost
If it is love, it will bring
All you thought you lost.

If it is love, with yourself start
Your own love you deny
Conditions set on your heart
That you are not worthy is a lie.

You have come to believe
You will deserve if you fix that or this
Yourself you do deceive
And a great love you do miss.

Set yourself completely free
Love your flaws and mistakes
Love all you might be
Love yourself before another day breaks.

November 3

What is the one thing that gets you up every morning? The one thing that keeps you going every day, every month, every year? Let me get you started. My one thing is this, "I'm one day closer..." One day closer to a goal, an outcome, or the results I'm after in my life. This is my way of remembering the importance of focusing on the life I desire and living a life of gratitude! So, what's your one thing...?
—James A. Murphy

I am not free from the darkness that often consumes me.

But again today I shall walk toward the light.

I am not free from the fears that often haunt me.

But again today I shall seek my courage.

I am not free from the chains that often take hold of me.

But again today I shall try another key.

I am not free from the pain that often settles over me.

But again today I shall allow myself to heal.

I am not free from the questions that often overwhelm me.

But again today I shall listen for my answers.

I am not free. But again today I am one day closer.

November 4

Wherever you are, be all there.
—Jim Elliot

Be present.
This space has a purpose.
Find it.

Be content.
This place has something to offer.
Accept it.

Be willing.
This time has lessons.
Be open to it.

Be mindful.
This feeling has meaning.
Understand it.

Be calm.
This question has an answer.
Listen for it.

Wherever you are, be all there.
For there is something waiting there for you.
Trust it.

November 5

Our lives improve only when we take chances. And the first and most difficult risk we can take is to be honest with ourselves.
—Walter Anderson

Comes a time to face fact
To finally drop your guard
Stop putting on an act
No matter how hard.

Behind the mask you hide
Hoping no one will know
The hurt that lives inside
Painful places that you go.

Days pass, and you fake
As if everything is OK
Still paying for a past mistake
It doesn't have to be this way.

We have all been broken
But we begin to heal
When our truth is spoken
And forgiveness we feel.

The truth waits silently
It knows why you are here
It is simply your story
You need no longer fear.

Look yourself in the eye
Say what you need to say
Softly kiss the past good-bye
Today is a new day.

November 6

I am realistic—I expect miracles.
—Wayne W. Dyer

Perhaps I am just an optimist.
For I believe in the positive, the possible, the beauty of this life.

Perhaps I am just a dreamer.
For I believe in miracles, the power of hope, and dreaming big.

Perhaps I am just naïve.
For I believe in the goodness, dignity, and resolve of the human spirit.

Perhaps I am just a hope-filled romantic.
For I believe in true love, happily ever after, and love's ability to heal.

Perhaps.

November 7

*It is when I struggle that I strengthen. It is when challenged
to my core that I learn the depth of who I am.*
—Dr. Steve Maraboli

I have known the struggle
Felt the sting of loss
Tasted tears of regret
Yet I faced the challenge.

Darkness invaded my soul
Demons haunted my days
Ghosts appeared before me
Yet I reached for the light.

The weight rested heavily
A load too great to bear
My spirit it sought to collapse
Yet I bore it with grace.

My path filled with detours
On my way to becoming
Took many a wrong turn
Yet I found my way home.

Failures have humbled me
Mistakes litter my story
I have stumbled often
Yet I still rise.

You have been given this life, complete with struggles and challenges, because you are strong enough to live it.

November 8

Breathe. Let go. And remind yourself that this very moment
is the only one you know you have for sure.
—Oprah Winfrey

Remind me again
Of where I'm heading
Of where I've been
This day I'm not dreading.

Remind me once more
Of all that I can do
Today is an open door
A chance to begin anew.

Remind me of my goal
Of how far I've traveled
Today I shall pay the toll
That dreams do not come unraveled.

Remind me of my strength
All the burdens I can lift
Today I go to any length
To know this day is a gift.

Remind me to stay present
Each moment defines me
May today truly represent
How and who I want to be.

November 9

Nothing ever goes away until it has taught us what we need to know.
—Pema Chodron

It simply waits.
Perhaps it hides in the darkness.
Only to softly whisper while you sleep.

It simply waits.
Perhaps it is tucked neatly away.
And although invisible, it makes its presence known.

It simply waits.
Perhaps it appears grand before you, as a wall or locked door.
Only you ignore it as if it were not there.

Whatever "it" is in your life, regardless of where or how it exists, it will not go away.
It waits to teach you the lesson.

Stop hiding, denying, and ignoring it.
Sit with it. Study it. Learn from it.
Only then will it go away.

November 10

*So this is the part where I'm supposed to tell you it's not scary. Well, it
is. But fear is natural, fear is good. It just means you're growing.*
—Unknown

Different is kind of scary.

Change is scary.

Letting go is pretty scary.

Not knowing is really scary.

And it is OK to have those fears.

It is a natural reaction.

Be OK with the trembling.

Learn to breathe with the nerves.

Enjoy your quickening pulse.

And then take the leap into the unknown.

For just beyond our fears lies our growth.

What we often do not realize is that fear is just a way of signaling to us that we are
standing at the edge of something wonderful—that something amazing awaits.

November 11

You know you're in love when you can't fall asleep because reality is finally better than your dreams.
—Dr. Seuss

In case you have not yet recognized, I'm in love.

So in love with...

The beauty of a new dawn breaking
For my breath it is taking.

The sun kissing my face to start each day
For it sets me on my way.

The aroma of the fresh morning breeze
For it smells of endless possibilities.

The simple sound of laughter
For it speaks of happily ever after.

The many blessings I have been given
For they are the gifts of simply livin'.

The time stepping away from the race
For it allows me to reset the pace.

The challenge set before me
For it is how I grow to be.

The moments spent on my knees
For it reminds me to say thanks and please.

The crooked, broken road I am navigating
For it leads to a dream I'm anticipating.

In case you have not yet recognized, I'm so in love...with my everything.

November 12

Live today. Not yesterday. Not tomorrow. Just today. Inhabit
your moments. Don't rent them out to tomorrow.
—Jerry Spinelli

Dear Tomorrow,

I know you are waiting for me to arrive. I hear you whisper my name. I feel you reaching out to me. I know you are out there, and I am longing to see you. As if an ache within me only you can ease.

But please know there is much I must do today so that I am ready for you.

I must take the lessons put before me today so I do not repeat the mistakes of yesterday.
I am still learning to be the best version of me.

I must allow today to free me so I do not bring the burdens of my past to you.
I am cleaning out the baggage, for you have no space for it.

I must quiet the voices of fear and doubt I listen to today so I can hear the truth of my story.
I am growing strong enough to be with you.

I must come to understand my value today so I do not discount what I have to offer you.
I am finding myself worthy of deserving you.

I must fill myself with light and love and hope today so I do not arrive empty.
I am wanting to bring these gifts to you.

I know you are out there. I know you are waiting. Please be patient with me. I will
arrive.

There are just some things I must do today.

Love, Me

November 13

Can a man still be brave if he's afraid? That is the only time a man can be brave.
—George R. R. Martin

I fear not the test
I fear never learning the lessons

I fear not the unknown
I fear never moving past what I know

I fear not being broken
I fear never knowing my strength

I fear not love saying good-bye
I fear never welcoming it in

I fear not the fall
I fear never taking the leap

I fear not the pain
I fear never exceeding my comfort

I fear not the dying
I fear never having lived

I fear not just anything
I fear never having my everything

Some know fear
And it paralyzes them.

Some know fear
And it frees them.

November 14

*When the seasons shift, even the subtle beginning, the scent of
a promised change, I feel something stir in me. Hopefulness?
Gratitude? Openness? Whatever it is, it is welcome.*
—Kristin Armstrong

I welcomed hope
It allowed me to see
Beyond this moment
And I feared less

I welcomed gratitude
It allowed me to see
All the many blessings
I had often overlooked

I welcomed openness
It allowed me to see
Into the dark corners
Places needing change

Something stirs in me
And I shall welcome it
Trusting what may come
For this is my season.

November 15

Running, you should know, is a kind of stillness.
—Tiphanie Yanique

Ran, thinking I was lost
Only to finally find myself
Ran with nowhere to go
Ended up coming home

Ran to escape the hurt
Learned to embrace pain
Ran so full of doubt
Emptied all the fear

Ran, believing I couldn't soar
Came to trust my wings
Ran without faith
Now only hope remains

Ran upon a broken road
Straight unto the healing
Ran amid the chaos
Suddenly there was calm.

November 16

All human wisdom is contained in these two words—Wait and Hope.
—Alexandre Dumas

I stood in my darkness
Patience and hope
My only companions
A light again returned

I sat with my pain
Patience and hope
My only comfort
Healing soon began

I wandered along my road
Patience and hope
My only signposts
The way became clear

I fought my demons
Patience and hope
My only protection
The peace settled in

I paid for my regret
Patience and hope
My only currency
Forgiveness freed me

I waited in my silence
Listening for an answer
Came a whispered hush,
"Wait and hope."

November 17

When you know what you want, you go toward it. Sometimes you
go very fast, and sometimes only an inch a year. Perhaps you feel
happier when you go fast. I don't know. I've forgotten the difference
long ago, because it doesn't matter, so long as you move.
—Ayn Rand

Dear Child,

Where are you going in such a hurry?
Can you sit awhile with me?
I promise I won't keep you long.

I know something calls to you.
And you must go toward it.
But must you always rush, my friend?

Have you taken time to simply exhale?
To slow your pace and look around?
You've come so very far.

Can you simply soak in the beauty and wonder of your journey?
Can you sit in the silence and listen to the strength of your beating heart?
Can you worry less about how fast you will arrive and know that you are on your way?

I know you will keep moving.
But I hope you never lose the rhythm of your dance.
I wish you peace as you go.

November 18

No one can save us but ourselves. No one can and no one may.
—Buddha

I dug this hole
With my own two hands.
As I place no blame
I fill the empty space.

I walked this path
With my eyes fully open.
As I own my steps
I change the course.

I brought this doubt
With the mind of one who did not trust.
As I learn to believe
I find the truth.

I broke this heart
With the darkness from within.
As I seek my light
I began to heal.

I lived this life
With my mistakes and regrets.
As I forgive myself
I begin to live again.

I alone save myself.
No one else can.
No one else may.

November 19

These are the days that must happen to you.
—Walt Whitman

These are the days
When pain returns
To steal your breath
One more time

These are the days
Breaking seems near
Closing in on you
Please not again

These are the days
Darkness calls to you
It is as if a thief
Daring to steal the light

These are the days
That must happen to you
So you finally know
They did not win

Dear, sweet friend
You are still breathing
You are not broken
Your light still shines.

November 20

Your heart is a weapon the size of your fist. Keep fighting. Keep loving.
—Leah Wilson

I hear a sound to get me through
It is the constant beating of my heart.

I own a light that sees me past the dark
It is the spark burning in my heart.

I possess a gift to heal the scars
It is the forgiveness held in my heart.

I have a weapon to combat the hate
It is the love that lives in my heart.

I know a place the best of me lives
It is in the quiet corners of this heart

November 21

Today I am in control because I want to be. I have my fingers on the switch, but have lived a lifetime ignoring the control I have over my own world. Today is different.
—A. S. King

Dear Today,

I will greet you with arms wide open and embrace you as you are.

I will honor you by not looking to yesterday nor rushing ahead to tomorrow.

I will be grateful for both the challenges and blessings you bring.

I will not offer you excuses; I will simply do my best for you.

I will trust the course you set for me.

I will use this time given me to learn, dance, explore, grow.

I will be all in, offering my 100 percent.

I will value you as the gift you are.

I will live and love you as though you are my first, as though you'll be my last.

This I promise you.

Love, Me

November 22

Those who dream by day are cognizant of many things
which escape those who dream only by night.
—Edgar Allan Poe

Dream wide awake
So others may see the light toward which you are walking.

Dream out loud
So others may hear the passion that calls out your name.

Dream insatiably
So others may taste the sweetness for which you thirst.

Dream from the heart
So others may feel that for which your pulse quickens.

Dream the impossible
So others will know how you will make it possible.

When you awake today, dream, my friend.
Dream.

November 23

Thanksgiving was never meant to be shut up in a single day.
—*Robert Caspar Lintner*

As I arrive at tomorrow's door
I shall cherish what's in store
So very much to be grateful for

My beautiful children
Everywhere I've been
Simply saying amen

My Sunday dances
My many second chances
Life's little circumstances

Family and dear friends
Laughter that never ends
Where life's road bends

The rising of the sun
The lesson of every run
That I am not yet done

All of the little things
That my heart still sings
All that gratitude brings

A life filled with love,
Life, and the mystery of
Simply all of the above.

464

November 24

Some people never take a chance and never know what it's like to live life to the full.
—Chloe Thurlow

I did not arrive here by chance
Luck played not a part
I cannot blame happenstance
'Twas a choice of the heart

I did not arrive here unknowingly
Did not stumble upon this place
Chose the destination I would see
When I decided to join the race

I did not arrive here without fears
It was not to be an easy road
A trail of blood, sweat, and tears
These were the tolls I owed

I did not arrive here unbroken
Walls and limits overcome
Within me something awoken
Refused to be comfortably numb

I did not arrive here unplanned
Mapped out a specific course
Then chose to take a stand
I will live my life full force.

November 25

How strange that the nature of life is change, yet the nature of human beings is to resist change. And how ironic that the difficult times we fear might ruin us are the very ones that can break us open and help us blossom into who we were meant to be.
—Elizabeth Lesser

If I am ever to find out what I am made of
I must tear myself completely open.

I must open the shadowy places.
The darkness within
Where I have feared to shed a light.

I must open the unexplored places.
The unknown within
Where I have feared to look.

I must open the vulnerable places.
The weakness within
Where I have feared to let go.

I must open the shattered places.
The truly broken within
Where I have feared to touch.

If I am ever to find out what I am made of
I must fear not what I find.

November 26

Everything you can imagine is real.
—Pablo Picasso

I wonder where my imagination has led me.

I wonder all that which I have made real for the images I have conjured in my mind.

How I breathed life into my fears
Until they were demons devouring my dreams.

How I sowed the seeds of my worry
Until they were the garden of my undoing.

How I fanned the flames of my doubts
Until they were my own living hell.

But, my friends, as I once brought my fears and worries and doubts to life
So, too, can I imagine a life without them.

I still battle my demons, but I know in my mind that they shall be slayed.

I still feel the thorns, but I know in my mind that they shall yield the rose.

I still dance among the flames, but I know in my mind that they shall be extinguished.

November 27

I must say a word about fear. It is life's only true opponent. Only fear can defeat life.
—Yann Martel

There are questions for which I do not possess answers.
I do not fear the test.
This is trust.

There are tasks I know not if I can complete.
But I do not fear the challenge.
This is faith.

There are mountains I am not sure I can scale.
But I do not fear the climb.
This is belief.

There are limits I wonder if I will ever overcome.
But I do not fear the wall.
This is strength.

There are paths down which I cannot see the ending.
But I do not fear the journey.
This is life.

November 28

True freedom is impossible without a mind made free by discipline.
—Mortimer J. Adler

Motivation wanes
Discipline endures

Motivation is fool's gold
Discipline pays the bills

Motivation has an expiration date
Discipline doesn't keep track of time

Motivation is a truth of convenience
Discipline won't listen to your lies

Motivation fails when it gets tough
Discipline succeeds despite the trial

Motivation. Discipline.
One is a way to get there.
One is a way of the warrior.

Be a warrior.

November 29

You are imperfect, permanently and inevitably flawed. And you are beautiful.
—Amy Bloom

Dear Life,

In case I have not told you lately, you are beautiful.

Beautifully complicated yet simple.

Beautifully ordinary yet extraordinary.

Beautifully fragile yet strong.

Beautifully imperfect yet perfect.

Beautifully mine.

In case I have not told you lately, you are beautiful.

It is how you arrive.

Love, Me

November 30

The world is not a place you live in; it is a place you change.
—*Pat Summit*

How do you change the world?

Offer a hand
Offer a smile
Offer a hug
Offer a prayer

Say please
Say thank you
Say I'm sorry
Say I love you

Stay kind
Stay humble
Stay gentle
Stay true

Be a light
Be a friend
Be a listener
Be a safe place to land

Share joy
Share beauty
Share laughter
Share love

Take turns
Take the high road
Take less than you give
Take only what you need

Live simply
Live honestly
Live peacefully
Live gratefully

Love your children
Love your family
Love your life
Love yourself.

December 1

It is not as much about who you used to be, as it is about who you choose to be.
—Sanhita Baruah

I am not defined by my stumbles or failures or struggles but by how I choose to live in this moment. May it be with grace.

I am not defined by my thoughts or words or hopes but by how I choose to live in this moment. May it be with kindness.

I am not defined by my occupation or position or income but by how I choose to live in this moment. May it be with gratitude.

I am not defined by my appearance or scars or imperfections but by how I choose to live in this moment. May it be with beauty.

I am not defined by my flaws or mistakes or faults but by how I choose to live in this moment. May it be with forgiveness.

I am not defined by my yesterday or tomorrow or future but by how I choose to live in this moment. May it be with love.

I am defined by how I choose to move from moment to moment. May it be in such a way as to always honor who I am.

December 2

Stress is caused by being "here" but wanting to be "there."
—Eckhart Tolle

You are where you need to be
A lesson here you need to see
Find the calm where you stand
Peace is found right at hand.

Trust what happens here
It may bring fear, cause a tear
Yet whatever comes today
Strengthens you in every way.

There can wait; it will arrive
But here you need to thrive
No promise can there give
Here is where you should live.

Trust more, worry less
In the moment find happiness
Stress not, believe more
Right here you can soar.

December 3

Will your eyes still smile from your cheeks?
—Ed Sheeran

These eyes have seen darkness, and still they smile.
For I always held firm to the light.

These eyes have seen storms, and still they smile.
For I always searched for the rainbow.

These eyes have seen tears, and still they smile.
For I always remembered the joy.

These eyes have seen hard days, and still they smile.
For I always understood better days would arrive.

These eyes have seen brokenness, and still they smile.
For I always knew it was just a part of becoming whole.

These eyes have seen lonely roads, and still they smile.
For I always trusted they would lead me home.

These eyes have seen love walk away, and still they smile.
For I always believed it would one day return to stay.

These eyes. Still they smile. Always.

December 4

Worry is most often a prideful way of thinking that you have more control over life and its circumstances than you actually do.
—June Hunt

This, another life chat.

Me: I'm not where I want to be.
Life: Do not worry; you will arrive on schedule.

Me: Here is not where I long to be.
Life: Do not worry; here holds something for you.

Me: Something out there is calling me.
Life: Do not worry; it knows you are coming.

Me: What if I do not get there in time?
Life: Do not worry; what you want will be waiting.

Me: I still want to be there, not here.
Life: Do not worry; the lesson you take from here will help you arrive.

Me: What is this lesson I am to learn here?
Life: Do not worry.

December 5

The most important things are the hardest to say because words diminish them.
—Stephen King

I hope this very day
I lived the words I long to say
I hope the way I walk
Matches the way I talk.

I fumble for words that say "I care"
May my actions let you know I'm there
I may grow silent when you are not OK
But I will hold your hand this day.

The words I do not always find
If you could only read my mind
Since you have no way of knowing
Let me start by simply showing.

Let me live every single day
So when I have words to say
You will know they are true
Because they are what I do.

December 6

And now that you don't have to be perfect, you can be good.
—John Steinbeck

In seeking perfection, my mistakes were amplified.
"You are not good enough," they cried.

In seeking perfection, paid such a cost.
The heart of who I am was confused and lost.

In seeking perfection, no time to pause.
Too much time spent hiding my flaws.

In seeking perfection, so much did slip away.
No time for living, no time for play.

And then the dawn did break.
I did not crumble when I made a mistake.

And in my imperfection I was able to find
Forgiveness and peace of mind.

I am forever flawed, yet perfectly me.
Finally able to clearly see.

To be good is all I need.
Comes the knowing, I have been freed.

December 7

Sometimes letting things go is an act of greater power than defending or hanging on.
—*Eckhart Tolle*

I feared the letting go.
Afraid of the loss.
Scared of the falling that would come.
Terrified of the pain that would ensue.

Desperately held on.
Grasping.
As a drowning victim.
Never knowing 'twas a stranglehold.

Thus, I let go.
Came the loss.
But more was gained.
The fall came hard.
But still I rise.
The pain blistering.
But comes the healing.

For in letting go
I found the power to bear that which I did so fear.
And in letting go, I took hold of my life line.

December 8

I cannot tell you any spiritual truth that deep within you don't know
already. All I can do is remind you of what you have forgotten.
—Eckhart Tolle

There is beauty in you
Rare and true
You must have forgot
Yet I have not.

You are a gift so rare
Handle with care
You must have forgot
Yet I have not.

You are a brilliant light
Shine so bright
You must have forgot
Yet I have not.

You are worthy
All should see
You must have forgot
Yet I have not.

These are truths of your spirit
Your soul longs to hear it
Remind yourself of what is true
Of all the things you once knew.

December 9

You don't drown by falling in the water. You drown by staying there.
—Edwin Louis Cole

You were pulled under.
The waves crashed over you.
Believed you were drowning.

You were pulled apart.
Dreams shattered around you.
Believed you were breaking.

You were knocked down.
Life had beat you up.
Believed you were weak.

You were cut deep.
Your heart laid open.
Believed you were bleeding.

You were left behind.
The past forgot you, the future you could not see.
Believed you were lost.

Sometimes, my friends, what we believe is not real.

You are not drowning.
You are learning to swim.

You are not breaking.
You are being rebuilt.

You are not weak.
You are growing stronger.

You are not bleeding.
You are healing.

You are not lost.
You are simply finding yourself.

December 10

If you don't give yourself permission to create a new
world, chances are nobody else will.
—James Altucher

Stamp your permit
To go for it
This day to be brave
Your life you can save.

Know no submission
Grant yourself permission
To be finally be free
To be truly happy.

Stare fear in the eye
You have permission to try
Take your foot off the brake
Your courage waits to awake.

No one can grant this for you
Only you can decide what to do
Brave enough to face the pain
Brave enough to let loose the chain.

Bound by fear for too long
Time to embrace your strong
A life controlled by doubt
Allow yourself to let it out.

Life can be so very tough
But you are brave enough
Brave enough to get up once more
Brave enough to face whatever is in store.

Stamp this day: permission granted
Seeds of courage already planted
They have just been waiting to grow
Until you allow yourself to go.

December 11

Happiness is like a butterfly which, when pursued, is always beyond our grasp, but which, if you sit down quietly, may alight upon you.
—Nathaniel Hawthorne

Perhaps happiness is not to be pursued
Maybe it simply arrives
As each day is renewed
If we are willing to open our eyes.

Perhaps happiness is not to be measured
Maybe it simply will overflow
Meant to be treasured
If we accept it as so.

Perhaps happiness is simply in you
Just begging for permission
To burst forth and anew
To its pleas will you listen?

Perhaps happiness has always been here
Maybe it never went away
May you wake to find it near
In your heart may it stay.

December 12

Life is a balance of holding on and letting go.
—Rumi

Comes a time to let go
Of that never meant to be
What it is, you already know
As you let go, you are free.

Comes a time to hold on
Of what you know is true
That which will never be gone
Hope, strength, dreams anew.

Comes a time to decide
What is worth the fight
And what to cast aside
Comes darkness or the light

To let go you must be brave
Trust your heart will be OK
Hope is a branch that will save
Hold on tightly this day.

December 13

There are days I drop words of comfort on myself like falling leaves
and remember that it is enough to be taken care of by my self.
—Brian Andreas

To yourself speak kind
Allow words to comfort
To end the war in your mind
And begin to heal the hurt.

Each word spoken
You hear every one
Time the chain broken
Negative talk now done.

Take care of you
'Tis where it must start
It is long overdue
Go easy on your heart.

You deserve your care
To others you give so much
With yourself begin to share
The same loving touch.

December 14

Everything you need is already inside.
—Bill Bowerman

That which you seek
Can easily be found
When inside you peek
Instead of looking around

When facing a test
Answers you don't know
Beating inside your chest
The heart knows where to go

When it is difficult to succeed
Something exists deep inside
The fuel for what you need
A simple little thing called pride

When the road gets rocky
Every mile seems uphill
The other side you will see
Because of your iron will

When failure comes calling
And you just want to quit
What keeps you from falling
Your indomitable spirit

When life comes hard
Looking to exact a toll
You hold the trump card
An unbreakable soul

Everything exists inside
When the questions begin
Answers no longer hide
Simply search from within.

December 15

Happiness cannot be far behind a grateful heart and a peaceful mind.
—Anonymous

I opened my heart to all that I am grateful for.

The love of family, company of good friends, kindness of strangers, comforts of home, satisfaction of a good day's work, health to see me through.

And my heart was overwhelmed with happiness.

I cleared my mind of all that makes it weary.

Worry of that I cannot change, stress over that I wish to happen, angst for what I do not know, fear of failing.

And my mind was freed to embrace all that which makes me happy.

Have gratitude in your heart and peace in your mind.

Happiness will find you.

December 16

*We were meant to live courageous and bold lives and not
lives of mediocrity. However, we have to live our lives actively
and on purpose each day to be unstoppable.*
—Thomas Narofsky

Today I will be completely free
Courage despite the fears
I will be the unstoppable me
I shall lead my own cheers.

Today I will get it done
I am an unstoppable force
Upon a path toward the sun
I set my very own course.

Today I shall be fiercely me
Whether wrong or right
I shall let others see
Nothing can dim my light.

Whatever is my goal
Fierce forward I shall go
Excuses will not take a toll
Failure I shall not know.

My challenge never too large
For I know where I want to be
Of my destiny I'm in charge
I will be the unstoppable me.

December 17

I am not a product of my circumstances. I am a product of my decisions.
—Stephen Covey

I am not confined by the circumstances of my life.
I am defined by the choices I make.

I am not a victim of the circumstances in my life.
I am a champion for facing every challenge laid before me.

I am not weak for the circumstances that have cut me down.
I am stronger for having risen every single time.

I am not bitter for the circumstances that may have soured my belief.
I am reaping the fruits for having kept the faith.

No event, not one person, past or present, determines who you are.
You are the product of your decisions.

Choose to be the best you that you can be.

December 18

My sun sets to rise again.
—*Robert Browning*

Come the darkness and shadows
Do not fear as the light fades away
For your heart surely knows
The darkness will not stay

I know you have felt the sorrow
Going on seems a difficult chore
Just as the sun comes up tomorrow
You, too, shall rise once more

Despite the fading light
And ever-rising doubt
You must not lose sight
You will find a way out

The darkness shall not last
If you keep hope within
Trust the strength you've amassed
Your light will always win

The sun will rise again, my friend
As today again you will try
These troubled times will end
And all your tears shall dry

Peace, hope, prayers, light, and love, my friend.

December 19

What in your life is calling you, when all the noise is silenced, the
meetings adjourned...the lists laid aside, and the Wild Iris blooms
by itself in the dark forest...What still pulls on your soul?
—Rumi

Your life just stopped by
It paid a visit to see
What you were willing to try
Who you are going to be

Your life wants you to know
It's not a dress rehearsal
This is the one big show
There is no rewind or reversal

Your life is a journey
And you pick the dream
To do what will set you free
An amazing gift to redeem

Your life is a chance
Every day a new choice
To sit it out or dance
To be silent or find your voice

Your life just gave a call
Your soul to awaken
It asks you to risk it all
Fear to be overtaken.

Your life is calling
How will you answer?

December 20

*To laugh often and much; To win the respect of intelligent people and
the affection of children; To earn the appreciation of honest critics and
endure the betrayal of false friends; To appreciate beauty, to find the best
in others; To leave the world a bit better, whether by a healthy child, a
garden patch, or a redeemed social condition; To know even one life has
breathed easier because you have lived. This is to have succeeded.*
—Ralph Waldo Emerson

The measure of success
May not be what you achieve
But that you helped another through a mess
That you helped another to believe.

Maybe you truly succeed
When you fully understand
It's helping someone in need
It's offering a helping hand.

We meet many along the road
Most we pass unknowing
Today let us lighten a load
Help a stranger as they are going.

As you go through this day
When others enter your space
What shall they have to say?
Did you leave them in a better place?

Success is doing for others
Not always about me
We're all sisters and brothers
Simply struggling to be.

December 21

*Adventure is about what we do; not what we plan, strategize or dream
about. Adventure begins with "what ifs" and "why nots." What if I were to
step out to chase that dream? Why not take the first steps and see what
happens? When we step through the doorway of adventure our life is
suddenly worth the living. And we experience life as it was meant to be.*
—Kevin E. Beasley

What if you are too caught up in the chase?

Toward something you think you do not possess. Or from something you are trying
to avoid.

What if this place is where you are meant to reside?

Could you simply stand still long enough to count the blessings that exist right here?

What if you are supposed to feel exactly what you are feeling?

Be it overwhelming sadness or numbing pain. Be it giddy with love or pure happiness.

What if that feeling was meant to teach a lesson?

Could you simply sit with it, embrace it, not push it aside or bury it, long enough to
learn from it?

What if you are all you will ever need to be just as you are?

That you do not need to change or become or fix anything about yourself.

Could you simply fall in love with all of your perceived frailties, flaws, and scars and embrace the unique, brilliant, beautiful, wonderful you?

What if nothing is wrong? Could you simply breathe and be OK?

December 22

The fear of failure takes the joy out of living.
—Charles F. Glassman

We have come to fear failure.

To the point where our fear is so great that we allow it to keep us from finding our limits, trying new, being uncomfortable, daring to dare, dreaming big.

We have come to fear failure.

To the point where our fear is so great that we allow ourselves to settle, grow complacent, accept mediocre, soften, remain stationary.

We have come to fear failure.

To the point where our fear is so great that we do not recognize failure as a teacher, valuable lesson, motivator, breakthrough, trusted friend.

We have come to fear failure.

To the point where we no longer fear what we should be most afraid of. To never try. To never search. To never dream. To never fail.

December 23

Don't you know yet? It is your light that lights the world.
—*Rumi*

There is a light in you, my child
Radiant, warm, beautiful
And, oh, how you do shine
You cast away the shadows

There is a light in you, my child
Not as the moon and stars
Yet no less heavenly
For yours does not fade

There is a light in you, my child
Unique in all the universe
Fear not its brilliance
You are made to shine

There is a light in you, my child.

December 24

The adventure of life is to learn. The goal of life is to grow. The nature of life is to change. The challenge of life is to overcome. The essence of life is to care. The secret of life is to dare. The beauty of life is to give. The joy of life is to love!
—William Arthur Ward

I have been given this life.
How shall I spend this treasure?
On days filled with light, laughter, and love.

I have been given this life.
How shall I use this gift?
For goodness, kindness, and peace.

I have been given this life.
How shall I express gratitude for this blessing?
By being and giving the very best of me.

I have been given this life.
How shall I repay this debt?
With a smile on my face, a prayer on my tongue, a joy in my heart.

I have been given this life.
How shall I choose to live it?
As if it were my only dream.

December 25

*If love is the greatest gift of all—and I believe it is—then the
greatest privilege of all is to be able to love someone.*
—Laura Schroff

You offered to me
The gift of your light
And it shone brightly
In the dark corners of me

You offered to me
The gift of your strength
And it lifted me up
When I felt I couldn't go on

You offered to me
The gift of your kindness
And it filled empty spaces
Deep within my heart

You offered to me
The gift of your hand
And it gave me hope
That I never walk alone

You offered to me
The gift of your friendship
And it wrapped around me
Bringing comfort and warmth

You offered to me
The gift of your love
And in the echo of its song
I finally learned to dance.

These
The greatest gifts to offer
All year round
Wishing you a very merry Christmas.

December 26

I look at struggle as an opportunity to grow. True struggle happens when you can sense what is not working for you and you're willing to take the appropriate action to correct the situation. Those who accomplish change are willing to engage the struggle.
—Danny Dreyer

I read of your struggle.

And I learned how strong you are. And it taught me to stand again.

I read of your struggle.

And I learned how you continue to find your way. And it taught me to move forward.

I read of your struggle.

And I learned how you face your fears. And it taught me to be brave.

I read of your struggle.

And I learned how you refuse to quit. And it taught me to never surrender.

I read of your struggle.

And I learned how you are not broken. And it taught me I will be OK.

I read of your struggle.

And I learned how lonely the path can feel. And it taught me I am never alone.

I read of your struggle.

And I learned you are not the struggle.

December 27

Reach out, share your truth, tell someone, "This is who
I am. This is what I stand for. Hold me to it."
—Kamal Ravikant

Many times, I simply sit, observe, and listen.

And when I do this, I see and hear themes and patterns that swirl for many of us. For you.

So, today, I put together a few truths that I feel you may be looking for.

Perhaps some of these speak to you, resonate with you.

1. Time and effort are the two greatest allies of change. Invest the time, put forth the effort; change is inevitable. This truth can be applied to any situation in your life.

2. Answers are not always necessary. You go, you do, you move; the answers will become clear. It is in the standing still where we feel we need to know the outcome.

3. Do not simply be tied to the outcome. This is where the seeds of disappointment are nourished. Allow yourself the opportunity to appreciate and celebrate the process.

4. Make gratitude a priority. By simply being thankful, so many negatives simply disappear.

5. Stress and worry are a holding of your breath. Without breathing, it's hard to live. Exhale.

6. You need both hands open to receive a gift or a dream, which means you have to let go of something you tightly cling to.

December 28

Just do what must be done. This may not be happiness, but it is greatness.
—George Bernard Shaw

What did you leave unshared?
A gratitude.
A gift.
A light.
Spread it.

What did you leave unresolved?
A problem.
A wound.
An ache.
Fix it.

What did you leave untended?
A flame.
A love.
A dream.
Care for it.

What did you leave undecided?
An answer.
A plan.
A path.
Choose it.

What did you leave unsaid?
A truth.
An apology.
An "I love you."
Speak it.

Life is quite simple.
Simply do what needs to be done.

December 29

We must never be afraid to be a sign of contradiction for the world.
—Mother Teresa

It is not always easy to be me.
Different.
Unique.
Gifts misunderstood.
A beauty of my very own.

It is not always easy to be me.
Flawed.
Scarred.
Times unable to stand.
A history of falling and rising.

It is not always easy to be me.
Trapped.
Undefined.
Questions without answers.
A mind tormented.

It is not always easy to be me.
Dreamer.
Believer.
Filled with wonder.
A gentle heart in a violent world.

It is not always easy to be me.
Overlooked.
Cast aside.
Judged harshly.
A solitary fighter.

It is not always easy to be me.
But for the struggle, I have been revealed.
Gifted.
Strong.
Mindful.
Tender-hearted.
A warrior.

December 30

*You read and write and sing and experience, thinking that one day
these things will build the character you admire to live as. You love
and lose and bleed best you can, to the extreme, hoping that one
day the world will read you like the poem you want to be.*
—Charlotte Eriksson

This, an autobiography in six short chapters.

I. The road.
Long.
Broken.
Lonely.

II. The fears.
Real.
Imagined.
Paralyzing.

III. The lessons.
Difficult.
Painful.
Needed.

IV. The truths.
Many.
Hidden.
Revealed.

V. The challenge.
Trust.
Surrender.
Fall.

VI. The reward.
Peace.
Love.
Home.

This, the story of my life.

December 31

I am nothing special, of this I am sure. I am a common man with common thoughts and I've led a common life. There are no monuments dedicated to me and my name will soon be forgotten, but I've loved another with all my heart and soul, and to me, this has always been enough.
—Nicholas Sparks

Three years ago, a quiet, simple, humble, good-hearted man began a journey. At the time, he was a bit broken, a bit lost, a bit undone, and so very alone. So he packed up his truck and headed west with no particular place to go.

Perhaps confused, perhaps angry, perhaps simply in search of something or some-place he had never been before, he set himself to find it. For deep down, he knew things needed to change.

What needed to change? you might ask. How he viewed the world and his place in it. How he viewed life and the purpose for it. And, most importantly, how he simply viewed himself.

Along the road, he learned about this world. The kindness and wonder and light and goodness it has to offer. For so many greeted him during his travels. Not as a stranger, but as a friend they were meeting for the very first time. And it softened him. Made him realize these small gestures, these simple acts of love perhaps do not change the entire world, but they changed his.

Along the road, he learned about this life. The simplicity and beauty and magic and meaning of it. For when he lay beneath the stars, in the silence of his solitude, he could hear life speak its message. And it caught his attention. Made him realize life, for all its hardships and trials, does not want to break you; it simply wants to shape you into the very best version of yourself.

Along the road, he learned about himself. The gifts and flaws and strengths and frail-ties. For as he wandered alone, only his company to keep, he began to become his very best friend. And it changed him. Made him realize for so long he never viewed himself through loving eyes. And only when he did was he able to finally save himself.

The journey has not been easy, and it continues to this day. So much has changed over the course of those three years. Much has not.

A quiet, simple, humble, good-hearted man once again takes to the road. But gone are the confusion, the brokenness, the anger. He's still heading to a place he's never been before. A place of light and love, a place called home.

But today he travels as an agent of change, a source of kindness and hope and light. Today, he travels fully aware of his gifts and strengths and his own unique beauty. Today, he travels one day closer, certain of where he is going, completely in love... with his everything.

Go get today. ~G

Made in the USA
Columbia, SC
24 May 2020

98125986R00290